AFRICAN AMERICAN JOURNALISTS

Autobiography as Memoir and Manifesto

Calvin L. Hall

The Scarecrow Press, Inc.
Lanham, Maryland • Toronto • Plymouth, UK
2009

SCARECROW PRESS, INC.

Published in the United States of America
by Scarecrow Press, Inc.
A wholly owned subsidary of
The Rowman & Littlefield Publishing Group, Inc.
4501 Forbes Boulevard, Suite 200, Lanham, Maryland 20706
www.scarecrowpress.com

Estover Road
Plymouth PL6 7PY
United Kingdom

British Library Cataloguing in Publication Information Available

Library of Congress Cataloging-in-Publication Data

Hall, Calvin L., 1964–
  African American journalists : autobiography as memoir and manifesto / Calvin
L. Hall.
    p. cm.
  Includes bibliographical references and index.
  ISBN 978-0-8108-6930-1 (pbk. : alk. paper) — ISBN 978-0-8108-6931-8 (ebook)
  1. American prose literature—African American authors—History and criticism.
2. African American authors—Biography—History and criticism. 3. African
American journalists—Biography—History and criticism. 4. Autobiography—
African American authors. 5. African American authors—Intellectual life. I. Title.
  PS366.A35H35 2009
  070.92'396073—dc22   2009006052

♾™ The paper used in this publication meets the minimum requirements of
American National Standard for Information Sciences—Permanence of
Paper for Printed Library Materials, ANSI/NISO Z39.48-1992.
Manufactured in the United States of America.

To Mom and Dad
To Sonya, Phillip, Sammy, and Aunt Diane

Credits

Contents

Acknowledgments

THE DEPARTMENT OF COMMUNICATION at Appalachian State University allowed me to have the time to reshape and rethink this work. (And thanks to Archie for taking time out of his cleaning schedule to check on me while I worked in my office at ungodly hours.)

My thanks also to those who read this at its incipient stage, and those who offered to read, like Jane Morgan and others whose names are too numerous to mention. I have plenty of work for you yet to come.

Friends Dwuan and Audrey June, David Ikard, Erick and Michelle Benson, David Bulla, Yolanda Butler, Kathy Roberts Forde, Dan and Monica Haygood, Tiffany Locus, Kelly McBride, Harry Williams, Kimberly Williams-Moore, Howard and Juanita Spanogle, and Scott and Kelly Welsh provided support, encouragement, and advice—and sometimes just people to hang out with to keep me sane—during the times of fear, panic, and uncertainty.

Stephen Ryan at the Scarecrow Press also deserves thanks. You have much better authors under your aegis, but none more appreciative of the opportunity.

Introduction

"Unexamined Lives": The Study of African American Journalism Autobiography

I tell you that it is the greatest good for a human being to have discussions every day about virtue and the other things you hear me talking about, examining myself and others, and that the unexamined life is not livable for a human being.

—Socrates

OVER THE YEARS, JOURNALISM RESEARCH HAS TENDED to explore the nature of the profession using the methods of the social sciences, mainly quantitative approaches. This does not mean that no research has been done using the qualitative methods of the social sciences or the humanities, only that the quantitative approaches have been the preferred way of studying journalism. However, greater exploration of qualitative or humanistic approaches to journalism studies will allow scholars to carve out a significant pathway of scholarship into the three areas that I believe comprise scholarship into journalism: (1) the people involved in the journalistic enterprise, (2) the process involved in creating journalism, and (3) the products created by journalists involved in the process. This book explores those three areas by focusing on the first. By examining the life stories of the people involved in creating journalism products, we can see how journalists participate in the journalism and how the stories they produce are dictated by their experience. Here, I examine selected autobiographies written by African American print journalists Jake Lamar, Jill Nelson, Nathan

McCall, and Patricia Raybon in order to explore the synergistic relationship between race, class, gender, and journalism. By synergistic, I
mean to imply more than a simple interconnectedness; I mean to suggest that the interactions between race, class, gender, and journalism
in autobiography constitute something more than mere life stories. To
this end, I explore how the authors turn autobiography and memoir
into quasi-political documents that challenge the status quo in journalism by illuminating, through lived experience, newsroom practices
that have been detrimental to the kind of diversity that allows journalism to fully inform readers.

This is a study of journalism via the study of life stories. The memoirs
written by Lamar, Nelson, McCall, and Raybon are the focus of discussion because these journalists worked in white mainstream newsrooms,
and their autobiographies discuss their experiences in the newsroom.
Moreover, all four began working in the mainstream press in the 1980s,
well after the ten-year anniversary of the Kerner Commission Report.
Their memoirs are the first African American autobiographies written
by print journalists to be published in the final decade of the twentieth
century.

A discussion of the importance of and current state of newsroom
diversity, truth, objectivity, and memory serves to highlight concepts
that serve as part of the foundation of this study. Another concept that
will inform this study is standpoint theory, defined by Nancy Hartsock
as a means of providing a Marxist critique of the relationship between
gender and power in society.[1] Though standpoint theory has its origin
in feminist studies, it can be a useful theory in the studies of other underrepresented, un-empowered groups. We can, for example, examine
works by African Americans through the prism of standpoint theory
as a way of illuminating the effects of white hegemony on people of
color.

Autobiography has a place of priority and privilege among the narrative traditions of African Americans because, as William Andrews
says, autobiographies have historically been appropriated as a site from
which African Americans can confront sociopolitical realities and suggest ways of altering them.[2] They are a direct connection from African
Americans' sociopolitical location—the "standpoint" suggested by
feminist theorists Sandra Harding and Julia T. Wood, as well as Hartsock—to the rest of the world.

Standpoint Theory

Central to standpoint theory, or standpoint epistemology, is the use of the "socially situated nature of various knowledge claims as the basis for maximizing objectivity."[3] The result of this is a necessary redefinition of the term "objectivity" that involves letting go of the idea that biases can be eliminated. In this redefinition, life experience is incorporated into the structure of the scientific method. As a result, standpoint theory suggests a potential use for limited subjectivities in journalism.

But what is the effect of the nonexistence of true objectivity, as suggested in standpoint epistemology, on the truth with regard to life writing by journalists? Does the nonexistence of true objectivity make the truth less true somehow? Standpoint theory suggests not. Mark P. Orbe states,

> Standpoint refers to a specific societal position, the result of one's field of experience, which serves as a vantage point from which persons interact with themselves and the world. A standpoint is not simply a subjective position that is interested in promoting bias but an acknowledgment of the sense of being engaged within a specific field of experience.[4]

Moreover, oral historian Sandy Polishuk says of the process of writing autobiographies that "when the author of an autobiography tells less than the truth, that is what stands."[5] So the truth becomes what the author says it is, and it is up to the reader to trust the author to—in the words of Emily Dickinson—"tell all the truth" from his or her "standpoint." Even if the writer tells less than "all the truth," exploring areas around what we perceive as the truth can provide fruitful areas of study.

The purpose of standpoint theory, as articulated by feminist scholars, is not to explain a process inasmuch as it is to provide a critique of the power relations between men and women in society. In doing so, it lays the foundation for new ways of thinking about knowledge and being and for understanding the ways in which hegemonic domination is constructed. At the heart of standpoint theory is a critique of Marxist ideas about the nature of power, which posit that that class relationships are defined by an era's means of production. Eventually these relationships cease to be compatible with the developing forces of production. At this point, a revolution occurs and a new ruling class emerges. For Marx, the progress of history is driven by larger economic forces: the creation of material goods, products, and services.

In the Marxist view, social relations change as economic conditions change; those who have a greater understanding of the means of production can gain and maintain control of society. This is accomplished by manipulating and exploiting those who are not in control in such a manner that they act against their own best interests. In the end, the Marxist concept of history is defined by a series of class struggles, given form and meaning by changes in economic structure. The Marxist view of societal evolution through revolution focuses not on radical shifts, but instead on gradual shifts in the structure and nature of changes between classes.

However, Hartsock says that while Marxian theories of society are sufficient for discussing class relations, they are ultimately inadequate in accounting for gender or racial domination and their accompanying white and male supremacy.[6] In defining standpoint as an epistemological framework, she examines how gender-centric domination has been created and maintained and whether, as a result, the idea of domination has been skewed by men's domination of women.[7] Another of Hartsock's goals is to develop a theory that can provide a more complete understanding of the structural changes needed to create a more egalitarian society.

Furthermore, while a critique of power relations in a capitalist society—or, as Hartsock says, "the ways the exercise of power over others is constructed, legitimated, and reproduced"—provides the framework of Hartsock's argument for standpoint, at the heart of her argument is the concept of community.[8] In order to critique power, you have to explicate the notion of community, for "theories of power are implicitly theories of community."[9] Hartsock defines community as the "by-product of activities directed at other ends."[10] The result is a social synthesis in which people conflict with one another and associate with each other only in indirect ways, on the basis of (mainly economic) self-interest. Hartsock's notion of community has similarities to what Mary Louise Pratt calls a "contact zone," defined as "social spaces where cultures meet, clash, and grapple with each other, often in contexts of highly asymmetrical relations of power."[11] As a contact zone, community, then, becomes a socioeconomic as well as a sociocultural location; it is a site for mutually beneficial exchanges, as well as a site for conflicts between the empowered and the un-empowered, the exploiters and the exploited.

How, then, does the idea of standpoint emerge from these notions? To answer this question, let us return to Marx's theories. In *The Communist Manifesto*, Marx identifies two fundamental social classes, which are in conflict: the bourgeoisie, the ruling class who own the means of production; and the proletariat, those without ownership who have to sell their labor.[12] The proletariat are soldiers—and slaves—for whom distinctions of age and sex become meaningless.[13] But while trapped in a cycle of exploitation, the proletariat gain a useful view of social relations that will eventually lead them to usurp power from the ruling class.

Hartsock views the lives of women in much the same way that Marx views the lives of the proletariat. They "make available a particular and privileged vantage point on male supremacy, a vantage point that can ground a powerful critique of the phallocratic institutions and ideology that constitute the capitalist form of patriarchy."[14] Women's lives are a vantage point from which gender-focused power relations and the ideologies behind them can be critiqued and redirected in pursuit of a society in which power is not usurped, but shared. Further, Hartsock suggests that a feminist standpoint allows for an analysis of material culture in such a way that it "illuminates the reasons why patriarchal institutions and ideologies take such perverse and deadly forms and how both theory and practice can be redirected in more liberatory directions."[15]

Hartsock posits the following claims that define standpoint:

Material life (class position in Marxist theory) not only structures but sets limits on the understanding of social relations.

If material life is structured in fundamentally opposing ways for two different groups, one can expect that the vision of each will represent an inversion of the other, and in systems of domination the vision available to the rulers will be both partial and perverse.

The vision of the ruling class (or gender) structures the material relations in which all parties are forced to participate and therefore cannot be dismissed as simply false.

In consequence, the vision available to the oppressed group must be struggled for and represents an achievement that requires both science to see beneath the surface of the social relations in which all are forced to participate and the education that can only grow from struggle to change those relations.

As an engaged vision, the understanding of the oppressed, the adoption of a standpoint exposes the real relations among human beings as

inhuman, points beyond the present, and carries a historically liberatory role.[16]

Hartsock aims to define standpoint in order to outline new ways of
gaining knowledge, new ways of defining and informing rationality.
She also wants to redefine ways in which we view material culture, a
key component of Marxian theories of society. But for the purposes of
this study, it is her final claim—that standpoint is an "engaged vision"
that will eventually allow us to move beyond inhuman relations—that is
most important to this study of objectivity and life writing.

Published the same year as Hartsock's work, Alison M. Jaggar's *Feminist Politics and Human Nature*, explains the validity of the standpoint
concept:

> The standpoint of the oppressed is not just different from that of the rul-
> ing class; it is also epistemologically advantageous. It provides the basis of
> for a view of reality that is more impartial than that of the ruling class and
> also more comprehensive. It is more impartial because it comes closer to
> representing the interests of society as a whole; whereas the standpoint of
> the ruling class reflects the interests of one section of the population, the
> standpoint of the oppressed represents the interests of the totality in that
> historical period.[17]

As a result, standpoint offers a more inclusive view of society because
it draws from the sociocultural location of the oppressed. The underlying
assumption is that the oppressed have witnessed all the ways in which
people on every sociocultural level operate. "Contact zones" become sites
of experience and knowledge about the "totality" of the human experience that the oppressor cannot access because, as Jaggar writes, "the con-
dition of the oppressed groups is visible only dimly to the ruling class."[18]
The result of this "dimmed vision" is that those who are oppressed can see
more clearly the connections between the oppressed and the oppressor—
and, ultimately, can better interpret both standpoints because their own
standpoint includes the standpoint of the ruling class.[19] In short, standpoint becomes the type of second sight that W. E. B. Du Bois described
in *The Souls of Black Folk*. However, instead of lacking a "true self-
consciousness" that lets one see him- or herself only through the revelation of the "other world"—the standpoint of the privileged—standpoint
allows for a full consciousness that reveals the whole world.[20]

Feminist standpoint presents an apparent paradox: A more inclusive understanding of the world arises from a situated experience of knowledge. One cannot be completely objective and rational if one views knowledge from a particular societal location. To show how this paradox has been resolved in feminist theory, Sandra Harding describes feminist standpoint as one of three responses to this paradox.[21] She describes the basic ideas behind feminist standpoint as the argument that "men's dominating position in social life results in partial and perverse understandings, whereas women's subjugated position provides the possibility of more complete and less perverse misunderstandings."[22] Among the conflicts Harding sees with feminist standpoint includes the idea that it is difficult for those for whom the empirical gathering of knowledge is important to dedicate themselves to the belief that the social position of the subject should be factored into the results of research.[23] Moreover, there are the following questions:

Can there be *a* feminist standpoint if women's (or feminists') social experience is divided by class, race, and culture? Must there be Black and white, working-class and professional-class, American and Nigerian feminist standpoints? . . . Is the feminist standpoint project still too firmly grounded in the historically disastrous alliance between knowledge and power characteristic of the modern epoch? Is it too firmly rooted in a problematic politics of essentialized identities?[24]

What happens, then, is that if standpoint depends on definitions of community and sociocultural location, then it needs something against which to define itself. There must necessarily be a dominant perspective. Though standpoint comments on Marxism by proposing to engage in a quest for a more egalitarian means of power sharing and knowledge seeking, it does not provide the means by which the dominant perspective allows for power to be shared. Those privileged with power do not share it easily, if at all. New standpoints—whether based on the fault lines of gender, race, or class—must be presented as valid without being perceived as a threat to the prevailing one. Autobiography and memoir provide ways of showing that the lives of people who are members of groups situated outside the dominant perspective have currency and agency.

Race, Gender, and Standpoint

Standpoint theory is highlighted when Patricia Hill Collins summarizes particular components of black feminist thought. In her analysis of the components, she discusses how they have been expressed in historical and modern-day contexts. She posits that the four basic components of standpoint—its thematic contents, its interpretive frameworks, its epistemological approaches, and its significance for empowerment—have been shaped by a continually changing political context.[25] They are not simply static elements; they grow and change. Standpoint, as she describes it, is one of the features of black feminist thought that is situated in a particular sociohistorical background:

> Historically, racial segregation in housing, education, and employment fostered group commonalities that encouraged the formation of group-based, collective standpoint. For example, the heavy concentration of U. S. Black women in domestic work coupled with racial segregation in housing and schools meant that U. S. Black women had common organizational networks that enabled them to share experiences and construct a collective body of wisdom. This collective wisdom on how to survive as U.S. Black women constituted a distinctive Black women's standpoint on gender-specific patterns of racial segregation and its accompanying economic penalties.[26]

Black women's standpoint and its connection to social and historical contexts, then, are not intrinsically different from what Harding and Hartsock have defined. However, in black feminist thought, standpoint acknowledges *another* layer of oppression—an additional prism through which power is refracted and reflected. Black womanhood exists as a community within a community and another point of contact. This means that there are multiple sociocultural locations that can be interpreted through the standpoint of black women.

But Collins warns that "because group standpoints are situated in, reflect, and help shape unjust power relations, standpoints are not static."[27] Indeed, shared experiences of oppression among African American women may lead to "similar angles of vision that could lead to the formation of a shared group knowledge or standpoint. But then again, because of intra-racial conflicts, they may not."[28] Moreover, because of an understanding of black womanhood as being positioned

as an additional site of marginalization—race in addition to gender—
there exists the possibility of overessentializing the standpoint of African American women. Collins writes, "Although it is tempting to claim
that Black women are more oppressed than everyone else and therefore
have the best standpoint from which to understand the mechanisms,
processes, and effects of oppression, this is not the case"[29] Instead, the
standpoint of black women should be one of many standpoints that
are used to examine ways of knowing. It is but one of many communities—sociocultural locations, contact zones—from which we can gain a
fuller understanding of the world.

A study that examines workplace issues through feminist standpoint
theory is P. Y. Martin's analysis of narrative accounts from six women
about their experiences with and interpretations of men at work.[30]
In addition to using standpoint theory, Martin also employs critical
scholarship on men and masculinities to guide her study. She concludes
that men routinely work together to "mobilize masculinities" at work,
that men routinely conflate masculinities and work dynamics, and that
men are often only vaguely aware of mobilizing masculinities. Furthermore, women experience masculinities mobilization, especially when
combined with work, as harmful. Her discussion notes how the gender
institution facilitates men's masculinities-mobilizing behaviors and
shapes women's interpretations and experiences of these behaviors.[31]
While Martin's study examined standpoint and the workplace, Meenakshi Gigi Durham's study examines standpoint in media, specifically
journalism.

For Durham, standpoint is a useful way for journalists to take into
consideration the views of marginalized groups, and, as a result, advance journalism.[32] The result will be stories that more accurately reflect
the varied experiences of those they write about and of those who read
their work: "By adopting a standpoint epistemology . . . a reporter actually gains access to a concrete mechanism for incorporating the class
analysis of a story into its reporting, which can be used to counter a
common source of bias in current reporting."[33] Durham's reporting
paradigm has the reporter considering the views of others in the community from which he or she reports; it also places the reporter *in* the
story and allows the reader to see, from multiple points of view, the ways
in which the various positions on an issue have been structured along
the most significant "fault lines"—areas of sociocultural division that

shape lives, experiences, and social tensions in the United States: race, class, gender, generation, and geography.[34] Instead of being simply social constructions, news and newsworthiness become sociocultural constructions that emerge from American society's conception of its world via the interaction between people along its fault lines. Throughout this discussion, "standpoint" refers to sociocultural locations for African American men and women, as well as a collective African American standpoint that is inclusive of both, as it is used in an analysis of the autobiographical works of the selected African American journalists and in connection with their experiences in the culture of the newsroom.

Also informing this study are theories that analyze life stories circumscribed by what Maurice Wallace calls the "vast area of repression around which the self-conscious autobiographical subject is always skirting."[35] These ideas allow for exploration of the ways African American journalists have used the autobiographical form to tell their stories in connection with the ideas about newsroom culture that also inform the study.

In addition to theories about African American autobiography, the concept of the autobiographical manifesto as defined by Sidonie Smith also informs the discussion and serves as the framing narrative for each of the memoirs. Smith describes autobiographical manifestos as a political hybrid of antiautobiography that has recently emerged in women's literature. It is "[p]urposeful, bold, contentious," and "contests the old inscriptions, the old histories, the old politics, the *ancien régime*, by working to dislodge the hold of the universal through an expressly political collocation of a new 'I.'"[36] The autobiographical manifesto is a combative document whose purpose is to allow its subject to assert him- or herself in the locale of the universal subject. The subject appropriates a space in the central standpoint from which to report his or her experience.

Other autobiographical theories, specifically the concept of relational selves as articulated by Paul John Eakin and the aforementioned concept of autobiographical manifestos, will contribute to the exploration as well. Moreover, theories of newsroom culture will also serve as a location from which understanding of these journalism memoirs will take place. This is important because the newsroom is a particular culture that consists of what Edgar H. Schein describes as "elements of a group organization that are most stable and least malleable."[37] These elements—such as ideals, values, mores, and other culturally constructed knowledge—bind an organizational community together. Examining the ways journalists are socialized into the newsroom community contextualizes the experiences described by the African American journalists whose autobiographies are discussed here.

Theories of Autobiography

In order to arrive at an understanding of the roles autobiography can play with relation to the previously discussed theories, the genre should be explored in relation to its meaning, its function for the writer, and its connection to experience. To John Sturrock, an autobiography has a near-mystical significance. An autobiography is a certificate of experience that details the passage of a unique individual through time, inviting a reader into its pages via a "metaphysics of presence," which is an underlying understanding of sharing the writer's experiences.[38] The reader is made part of the writer's lived experience through the process of reading. However, the scholar of autobiography reads autobiography in order to dissect the life and gain knowledge from it, with much the same attitude, perhaps, as a biologist would dissect a lab specimen, looking for "formal or textual variety, . . . comprehensiveness[,]," or "generic sameness."[39]

Autobiographies are "retrospective prose written by a real person concerning his own existence where the focus is his [or her] individual life, in particular, the story of his [or her] personality," according to Phillipe Lejeune.[40] Autobiographies focus on how one person came to understand his or her own life. Lejeune references author John Updike's idea of the autobiography as a writer's way of coping with the "unbearable" knowledge that he or she is leaving behind multiple versions of him- or herself that may or may not be wholly representative of the person the writer really is—"dead, unrecoverable selves."[41] This idea overstates the case and makes autobiographers seem more concerned with how they are perceived by others than with wanting to leave messages for the world.

"All identity is relational," Eakin states, and the autobiography exists as more than the story of one life.[42] An autobiography is the story of how the self is created in relation to other "selves." The autobiographical subject is a "relational self" whose identity is formed in connection to, and in interaction with, other lives. Identities are not formed in isolation. They need the presence of other people shaping, directing, and conflicting with them. Thus, an autobiography is not a soliloquy of the self; it is dialogue and voice-over narration, individual and communal. The relational self becomes an individual standpoint informed by other individual standpoints. And autobiography is a way of reporting from those standpoints.

What other roles can autobiographies fulfill besides the communication of personal experience? According to the literature, they exist not simply to put a name with a life story, but to put a life story with a name.[43] The stories exist to give the writer an identity—but not just any identity. The writer receives the identity belonging to a particular story. We then associate that writer with that story, with that lived experience. In essence, an autobiographer says, "*Because* this happened to me, this is who I am," instead of "This is who I am, and this is what happened to me."

Autobiographies also serve to bring into consciousness that which was part of the writer's unconscious, so that the autobiographer can see how he or she arrived at a particular point in time.[44] And, because autobiographers record and preserve the inward feelings they had during particular times in history, autobiographies serve as artifacts for historians. Sturrock puts forth the idea that autobiographies serve as the story of singularity, of "how the autobiographer came to acquire the conviction of uniqueness that has impelled him—or her—to write."[45] For African American journalists of the modern era—such as Jill Nelson, Nathan McCall, Jake Lamar, and Patricia Raybon—that conviction has two sources: the nature of the concept of race in society and the nature of their profession.

Autobiographies also function as a means to explore the conflict between the "will to apartness" and the "will to association."[46] The autobiographer sees him- or herself as apart from others. Conflict stems from the fact that a life story is told because it sets its subject apart in some way, but the act of autobiography is itself one that has as its latent intent to connect the writer with others, those "others" being readers.

"Experience" in Autobiography and Journalism

How does experience function in relation to autobiography? Is experience simply the memory of past events? Joan Scott contends that it is not, that experience has particular components that cannot be explored by autobiography alone. Experience, she says, is "the start of a process that culminates in the realization and articulation of social consciousness."[47] This social consciousness is connected to the idea of "relational selves" in that it implies that an individual is formed by more than just his or her singular experiences. It is the interconnectedness with others that forms the foundation of what is to be a complete life. Experience—and evidence of experience—is simply the foundation for something higher. It "constitutes" subjects:

> It is not individuals who have experience, but subjects who are constituted through experience. Experience in this definition then becomes not the origin of our explanation, not the authoritative (because seen or felt) evidence that grounds what is known, but rather that which we seek to explain, that about which knowledge is produced.[48]

Instead of seeking knowledge about experience, we produce knowledge about experience, through autobiography—as well as through journalism. In the end, Scott says, "experience," as a word, is something that we—as readers, writers, and scholars—cannot do without. It is both "an interpretation and in need of an interpretation"; it is contested and therefore political.[49] In her definitions of "experience" and the meaning of "experience," Scott presents a strong case about the contested, political nature of experience. Her ideas provide a useful context for discussing African American autobiography because they illuminate the importance of the conflicted, contested nature of blackness.

The "Special Case" of African American Autobiography

Autobiography as a forum—despite what Robert Folkenflik called its "weak canonical status"—is connected to the possibility of civic unification:

> Part of the current appeal of autobiography has to do with its democratic potential, with its suggestion that each person has a possible autobiography allotted him or her, and with its connections to a "bottoms up" historiography that would enfranchise anyone ready to tell his or her tale (including orally). From this perspective, the weak canonical status of autobiography is an advantage, and its importance especially in recent years as a vehicle for members of minorities and inhabitants of third world countries is obvious.[50]

For the autobiographies written by African American journalists, the democratic potential of the autobiography has been in evidence throughout the history of African Americans and their involvement in the journalistic enterprise. At its most idealized, journalism itself could be considered a form of autobiography—an autobiography of a society written by empowered selves. For Frederick Douglass (publisher of the *North Star*) and W. E. B. Du Bois (editor of the *Crisis*), as well as Ida B. Wells-Barnett and Booker T. Washington, autobiography provided a forum for them to expand upon the journalistic activism characteristic of the black press. The journalism practiced by the black press was—and still is—a type of viewpoint journalism, speaking to a group on behalf of another group. Memoir and autobiography allowed early practitioners in the black press to step outside the role of spokesperson/sociocultural autobiographer in order to transmit their own individual life stories to an audience waiting to read them. Indeed, in the scope of black experience, autobiography has arguably been more important than journalism in reporting about the individual African American experience in the context of larger society. The memoirs that are the focus of this study reflect this.

Ultimately, modern autobiographies of African American journalists provide worthwhile sources for study because they are the best medium for African American journalists to tell how the experience of journalism has impacted African American journalists in a postmodern, post–civil rights movement world. They are part of a narrative tradition that, according to Jerome Bruner, has its origins in fugitive slave memoirs and continues through the accomodationist writings of Booker T. Washington, the contemplative confrontational writings of Douglass, and even into the works of literary authors like Richard Wright.[51] The power of these memoirs comes from the fact that they can make these origins clear while creating new texts that reflect all the ironies and the self-reflection inherent in the postmodern fictional sensibility.[52]

Despite the "psychological self-deceptions and constructions" they may or may not contain, autobiographies allow writers more complete control over the shape of their stories in a way that is not possible in other genres of life writing, such as oral histories, because they provide a less mediated experience.

Examining the autobiographies written by contemporary black journalists allows us to consider the possibility of connected relationships between categories such as race, class, gender, and profession. Journalism is the profession that provides a site for examination, primarily because of its supposed watchdog role on government and the belief of its practitioners in the concepts of fairness, accuracy, and balance. Moreover, key to understanding these autobiographies is in an understanding of two concepts defined by W. E. B. Du Bois in *The Souls of Black Folk*: "the veil" and "two-ness." In opening pages of *Souls*, Du Bois states that he wants to "sketch, in vague, uncertain outline, the spiritual world in which ten thousand, thousand, Americans live and strive."[53] This spiritual world is part of a social system of behavior in which "the Negro is a sort of seventh son, born with a veil, and gifted with second-sight . . . which yields him no true self-consciousness, but only lets him see himself through the revelation of the other world."[54] This presents a seeming contradiction wherein an oppressed people have second sight, but how and what they see is out of their control. What seems to be a blessing in second sight, then, becomes a useless ability. What good is the ability to perceive dualities when the holder of such ability depends on the interpretations of those who are not so gifted? Does the veil become an impediment to the quest for truth in the newsroom?

Furthermore, behind the veil, an oppressed people develop a double consciousness—a "two-ness." This two-ness is comprised of "two souls, two thoughts, two unreconciled strivings; two warring ideals."[55] How does this two-ness manifest itself within the aforementioned synergistic relationships? Because standpoint theory embraces the lived experiences of underrepresented groups, it is possible to engage in exploration of representations of "the veil" and "two-ness" in African American autobiographies.

In the end, the autobiographies of African American journalists function as more than mere life stories. They are documents in the public sphere, which Jürgen Habermas defines as "a network for communicating information and points of view," where "the streams of communication are, in the process, filtered and synthesized in such a way as that they coalesce into bundles of topically specified *public* opinions."[56] The public sphere is not so much a physical place as it is a social realm that developed within various structures. It exists as discourse and conversation that engages in a Socratic dialogue with institutions and is able to critique those institutions.

Scott says that visible group experiences expose the existence of systems of repression, but not how they work.[57] On this point, she may be mistaken. Exposing and describing the inner workings of repressive systems has been one of the purposes of autobiography in African American culture. This gives the text and the genre meaning, especially if the writer directly acknowledges his or her blackness. For example, Frederick Douglass's various versions of his *The Narrative of the Life of Frederick Douglass, an American Slave* not only describe his experience, they also expose the inner workings of the slavery—how it dehumanizes both slave and master.

Any African American with something to say about the nature of oppression African Americans have faced has, historically, used the autobiographical form as the means through which to say it. From the autobiographical writings of Douglass to William Wells Brown to Booker T. Washington, Ida B. Wells-Barnett, and W. E. B. Du Bois, the genre has been recognized and celebrated as a powerful means of speaking publicly about and changing the nature of the sociopolitical and cultural realities in America—in particular, the reality of what it means to be black in America.

Blackness, according to British cultural theorist Stuart Hall, has always been a psychically, culturally, and politically unstable identity,[58] in that it has continually needed—or has been forced to need—definition and delineation in a way that other group identities (gender, for example) have not. Moreover, blackness, at least in the Anglo-American democratic sense, has never just been "found," has never just been "there."[59] Likewise the production of black cultural identity has never been a complete process; it requires being constituted within representation.[60] As a result, blackness has a narrative, a history that must be constructed, shared, and spoken.

Where do the autobiographies written by African American journalists fit into the genre? How do they help define group identities? In short, they perform the same function African American autobiographies have always served: They speak publicly about the nature of a repressive system. But this time, the profession of journalism—as reflected by the corporate newsroom—is the system that is the focus of critique. I posit that African American journalists speak as one of a group, defining, on their own terms, the black workplace identity as constituted in the newsroom culture.

The stories of African American women journalists such as Jill Nelson have the added dimension of gender. Joanne M. Braxton states that

autobiographies written by black women have significance that transcends race and gender because black women are born into a mystical
sisterhood; they have been "knowers," but they have not been known
in the same way that white men, black men, and even white women
have been.[61] In short, their standpoints include the standpoints of the
marginalized as well as the nonmarginalized. African American women
journalists, like other African American women who write autobiography, use the form to contest the sovereignty of those who have been
known. They appropriate a space for themselves from which to present
their standpoints. Because of this, there exists the possibility that these
works—and the memoirs of African American male journalists—might
also serve as examples of autobiographical manifestos. Like standpoint
theory, the concept of the autobiographical manifesto has roots in
feminist studies, but contains implications for the study of other marginalized groups. These implications include providing a way of reading
autobiographical writing by members of marginalized groups that may
suggest new ways of looking at journalism studies.

The Discussion in This Text

The concept of the autobiographical manifesto will be the guidepost
along the way during the exploration of the memoirs of Jill Nelson,
Nathan McCall, Jake Lamar, and Partricia Raybon. After the first
chapter, which presents an overview of the nature of journalism with
the intention of contextualizing the place of memory, truth, objectivity, and autobiography in journalism, the succeeding chapters will
examine how the characteristics of the autobiographical manifesto
are present in four texts. Chapter 2 consists of an examination of
how the characteristics of the autobiographical manifesto are present in Jill Nelson's *Volunteer Slavery: My Authentic Negro Experience*,
with a particular focus on the place of the document in the public
sphere. Chapter 3 continues the discussion of Nelson's book by
focusing on the vocal aspects of the text. In chapter 4, I analyze the
autobiographical manifesto aspects of Nathan McCall's *Makes Me
Wanna Holler: A Young Black Man in America*, focusing mainly on
surveillance and performance. Because the memoirs of Jake Lamar
and Partricia Raybon are shorter than Nelson's and McCall's, they

are examined together in chapter 5, with a focus on form. Chapter 6 presents an exploration of the themes that emerge from the texts and their implications for African American journalists in relation to the newsroom culture. The text concludes by looking at the connections between race, class, gender, and profession in the autobiographies. Some may argue that an evaluation of the memoirs as autobiographical manifestos provides only a limited view of the texts; they may believe that critiquing them as simply manifestos robs them of their effectiveness. However, it is my belief that this is a narrow view of the declarative power of the memoir. Moreover, there is room for considerations of the professional memoir in many methodologically different ways, and I believe that this potentially provides a new way of looking at journalism. For those who are engaged in the journalistic enterprise as well as those outside of it, studies of life stories of other journalists will help them understand the perspectives of other journalists—particularly those from underrepresented groups—and how those life stories can be interpreted.

Notes

1. Meenakshi Gigi Durham, "On the Relevance of Standpoint Epistemology to the Practice of Journalism: The Case for 'Strong Objectivity,'" *Communication Theory* 8, no. 2 (1998).

2. William L. Andrews, *African American Autobiography: A Collection of Critical Essays*, New Century Views (Englewood Cliffs, NJ: Prentice Hall, 1993), 1.

3. Durham, "On the Relevance of Standpoint Epistemology to the Practice of Journalism," 117–40.

4. Mark P. Orbe, "Foundations of Muted-Group and Standpoint Theory," in *Constructing Co-Cultural Theory: An Explication of Culture, Power, and Communication* (Thousand Oaks, CA: Sage, 1998), 26.

5. Sandy Polishuk, "Secrets, Lies, and Misremembering: The Perils of Oral History Interviewing," *Frontiers—A Journal of Women's Studies* 19, no. 3 (1998): 22.

6. Nancy C. M. Hartsock, *Money, Sex, and Power: Toward a Feminist Historical Materialism*, Longman Series in Feminist Theory (New York: Longman, 1983), 1.

7. Hartsock, *Money, Sex, and Power.*

8. Hartsock, *Money, Sex, and Power*, 1.

9. Hartsock, *Money, Sex, and Power*, 3.

10. Hartsock, *Money, Sex, and Power*, 103.

11. Mary Louise Pratt, "Arts of the Contact Zone," *Profession 91* (1990): 34.

12. Karl Marx, Friedrich Engels, and Robert C. Tucker, *The Marx-Engels Reader*, 2d ed. (New York: Norton, 1978).

13. Marx, Engels, and Tucker, *The Marx-Engels Reader*.

14. Hartsock, *Money, Sex, and Power*, 231.

15. Hartsock, *Money, Sex, and Power*, 231.

16. Hartsock, *Money, Sex, and Power*, 232.

17. Alison M. Jaggar, *Feminist Politics and Human Nature*, Philosophy and Society (Totowa, NJ: Rowman & Allanheld, 1983), 370–71.

18. Jaggar, *Feminist Politics and Human Nature*, 371.

19. Jaggar, *Feminist Politics and Human Nature*, 371.

20. W. E. B. Du Bois, *The Souls of Black Folk* (Millwood, NY: Kraus-Thomson Organization, 1973), The Forethought.

21. Sandra G. Harding, *The Science Question in Feminism* (Ithaca, NY: Cornell University Press, 1986), 24. The other two are feminist empiricism and feminist postmodernism. Feminist empiricism posits that sexism is a social bias correctable by stricter adherence to the existing norms of scientific inquiry. Feminist postmodernism challenges the basic assumptions of feminist empiricism and feminist standpoint. According to Harding, "It requires seeking a solidarity in our oppositions to the dangerous fiction of the naturalized, essentialized, uniquely 'human' (read 'manly') and to the distortion and exploitation perpetrated on behalf of this fiction" (24–28).

22. Harding, *The Science Question in Feminism*, 26.

23. Harding, *The Science Question in Feminism*, 26.

24. Harding, *The Science Question in Feminism*, 26–27.

25. Patricia Hill Collins, *Black Feminist Thought: Knowledge, Consciousness, and the Politics of Empowerment*, rev. 10th anniversary ed. (New York: Routledge, 2000), 17.

26. Collins, *Black Feminist Thought*, 24.

27. Collins, *Black Feminist Thought*, 25.

28. Collins, *Black Feminist Thought*, 25.

29. Collins, *Black Feminist Thought*, 270.

30. P. Y. Martin, "'Mobilizing Masculinities': Women's Experiences of Men at Work," *Organization* 8, no. 4 (2001).

31. Martin, "'Mobilizing Masculinities.'"

32. Durham, "On the Relevance of Standpoint Epistemology to the Practice of Journalism," 132.

33. Durham, "On the Relevance of Standpoint Epistemology to the Practice of Journalism," 135.

34. Robert C. Maynard Institute for Journalism Education, "Fault Lines," www.mije.org/faultlines.

35. Maurice O. Wallace, *Constructing the Black Masculine: Identity and Ideality in African American Men's Literature and Culture, 1775–1995* (Durham, NC: Duke University Press, 2002), 84.

36. Sidonie Smith, "Autobiographical Manifestos," in *Women, Autobiography, Theory: A Reader*, ed. Sidonie Smith and Julia Watson, Wisconsin Studies in American Autobiography (Madison: University of Wisconsin Press, 1998), 435.

37. Edgar H. Schein, *Organizational Culture and Leadership*, 2nd ed. (San Francisco: Jossey-Bass, 1992), 5.

38. John Sturrock, *The Language of Autobiography: Studies in the First Person Singular* (New York: Cambridge University Press, 1993), 3.

39. Sturrock, *The Language of Autobiography*, 3.

40. Paul John Eakin, *How Our Lives Become Stories: Making Selves*, Cornell Paperbacks (Ithaca, NY: Cornell University Press, 1999), 77.

41. Eakin, *How Our Lives Become Stories*, 93.

42. Eakin, *How Our Lives Become Stories*, 43.

43. Sturrock, *The Language of Autobiography*, 5.

44. Sturrock, *The Language of Autobiography*, 6.

45. Sturrock, *The Language of Autobiography*, 14.

46. Sturrock, *The Language of Autobiography*, 18.

47. Joan Scott, "Experience," in *Feminists Theorize the Political*, ed. Judith Butler and Joan Scott (New York: Routledge, 1992), 30.

48. Scott, "Experience," 26.

49. Scott, "Experience," 37.

50. Robert Folkenflik, *The Culture of Autobiography: Constructions of Self-Representation*, Irvine Studies in the Humanities (Stanford, CA: Stanford University Press, 1993), 12.

51. Jerome Bruner, "The Autobiographical Process," in *The Culture of Autobiography: Constructions of Self-Representation*, ed. Robert Folkenflik, Irvine Studies in the Humanities (Stanford, CA: Stanford University Press, 1993), 50.

52. Bruner, "The Autobiographical Process," 50.

53. Du Bois, *The Souls of Black Folk*, The Forethought.

54. Du Bois, *The Souls of Black Folk*, The Forethought.

55. Du Bois, *The Souls of Black Folk*, 3.

56. Jürgen Habermas, "Civil Society and the Political Public Sphere," in *Contemporary Sociological Theory*, ed. Craig J. Calhoun, Blackwell Readers in Sociology (Oxford: Blackwell, 2002), 354.

57. Scott, "Experience," 25.

58. Scott, "Experience," 33.

59. Stuart Hall, "Minimal Selves," in *ICA Documents 6: Identity*, ed. Luisa Appignanesi (London: Institute of Contemporary Arts, 1987), 45.

60. Stuart Hall, "Cultural Identity and Diaspora," in *Identity: Community, Culture, Difference*, ed. John Rutherford (London: Lawrence & Wishart, 1990), 222.

61. Joanne M. Braxton, *Black Women Writing Autobiography: A Tradition within a Tradition* (Philadelphia: Temple University Press, 1989), 1.

1

Journalism:
Memory, History, and Context

<hr/>

IF PROJECTIONS BY THE U.S. CENSUS BUREAU ARE ACCURATE, the United States will be a lot less white by the middle of the twenty-first century. Bureau officials predict that by 2023, half of all children born in the United States will be members of racial and ethnic minority groups.[1] By 2042, ethnic and racial minority groups, which now comprise about a third of the nation's population, will make up the majority of its citizens. By 2050, 54 percent of the nation's population will be members of racial or ethnic minority groups.[2]

As American society becomes increasingly more diverse, the need for journalists of color becomes increasingly more important in helping newspapers illuminate the mosaic of cultures that make up American society. Journalism traffics in the "truth." According to Bill Kovach and Tom Rosenstiel, "The journalist's first obligation is to the truth."[3] But truth is an expansive, shifting, contested concept whose meaning even journalists are unsure about:

> Journalism by nature is reactive and practical rather than philosophical and introspective. The serious literature by journalists thinking through such issues is not rich, and what little there is, most journalists have not read. Theories of journalism are left to the academy, and many newspeople have historically devalued journalism education, arguing that the only place to learn is by osmosis on the job.[4]

According to Jack Fuller, the pursuit of truth in the journalistic enterprise has its origins in the Progressive Era ideal of disinterested judgment in the public interest that became the focus of important figures
in journalism in the early part of the twentieth century.[5] Later in the era,
as university training of journalists became more commonplace, the notion of newsgathering as a profession—rather than a trade—grew. This,
coupled with a decline in the number of newspapers serving individual
communities and surviving papers passing out of the control of the
founders and their families and into the hands of the corporate managers, led to the idea that journalism aspires to a higher standard of truth.[6]
Before the Progressive Era, publishers had always claimed sovereignty
over the truth, the whole truth, and nothing but the truth, but because
of the changes in the profession—in training, in ideas about gathering
information—journalists themselves eventually began to actually claim
it. "It was an important step," Fuller writes, "and a salutary one for the
quality of public discussion. But to this day, many of its implications
remain inadequately examined."[7]

If the practical, reactive nature of journalism keeps journalists from
understanding the full meaning of the concept of truth, then the newsroom setting is the only place where journalists can have the kinds of
instructive experiences that allow them to see that the truths they pur-
port to chronicle are often incomplete. Truth changes with perspective.
It changes with distance. Those closest to a subject may have a better
understanding of an aspect of the truth than someone claiming to view
it objectively, particularly on matters such as race. But journalists who
interact only with journalists whose beliefs and experiences are similar
to theirs never fully understand this idea. This is why it is important in
the coming years to ensure a racially diverse newsroom. The civil rights
movement of the 1950s and racial strife in the 1960s led to the integration of the newsroom staffs of mainstream papers. Black reporters were
needed in the mainstream to cover stories that white reporters could not
because, in some black communities, white reporters were harassed and
sources refused to talk to them.[8]

The struggle of African American journalists for inclusion in the
mainstream press originates from the desire of black people to have
control over the presentation of the images of and ideas about black
life. This was part of a strategy of racial uplift established by John Russ-
wurm and Samuel Cornish with the publication of *Freedom's Journal* in

1827, and the beginning of the black press in America. The stated goals of Russworm and Cornish, often quoted, were: "We wish to plead our own cause. Too long have others spoken for us. Too long have we been misrepresented in things that concern us dearly." [9] This is the legacy that the first African American journalists to enter white mainstream newsrooms, after the release of the Kerner Commission Report in 1968, were hired to uphold.[10]

The Kerner Commission had its genesis in the civil rights movement's pursuit of racial justice for blacks in the South that became a shared pursuit of the black and white press. But the Watts Uprising and the urban unrest that swept the nation from 1965 to 1968 served as the turning point for the agenda, leading to the formation of the Kerner Commission by President Lyndon Johnson in 1967. Among the directives of the commission, formally known as the National Advisory Council on Civil Disorders, were to find out why the uprising happened and what could be done to prevent similar incidents in the future.[11] In its section on the media, the report stated that the media's reporting on the disturbances was not the sole problem; problems also stemmed from the media's overall treatment of black ghettos, its poor community relations, and the negative racial attitudes of many media members, as well as the media's negative attitudes toward urban and rural poverty.[12]

The commission concluded that even though the media made an effort to give a balanced account of the event, it did not accurately present the scale and character of the Watts Uprising and actually exaggerated the nature of the happenings.[13] Moreover, local media failed to report enough about the causes of the events and focused too much on national events at the expense of reporting on race relations in its own backyard.[14] Because of the cumulative effect of negative associations and attitudes about black communities and individuals, the media failed to communicate adequate and representative information about the riots to citizens—black or white—concerning urban neighborhoods and crime and law enforcement.[15] The report stated that the media "simply must exercise a higher degree of care" in stories regarding race and unrest, perhaps more so than in many other kinds of stories.[16]

Of the recommendations the commission made for improved coverage of race issues in the United States, two are important to this project: the addition of more blacks to newsrooms as journalists and the recognition of African Americans in media coverage. Before the Watts

Uprising, the white press failed to cover African Americans as a normal part of American society; it failed to present to its audiences the severe problems faced by blacks, particularly those living in the urban ghettos; and it reflected indifference and antipathy toward blacks in its coverage, according to Carolyn Martindale.[17] These issues are addressed in the Kerner Commission Report:

> The media report and write from the standpoint of a white man's world. The ills of the ghetto, the difficulties of life there, the Negro's burning sense of grievance, are seldom conveyed. Slights and indignities are part of the Negro's daily life, and many of them come from what he now calls "the white press"—a press that repeatedly, if unconsciously, reflects the biases, the paternalism, the indifference of white America.[18]

While such reporting may be understandable, the report continues, it is not excusable in the media, an institution that has undertaken the mission of informing and educating the whole of society. It is said that the first step in fixing a problem is admitting the problem exists. In this acknowledgment of a particular standpoint in the reporting of the news, the Kerner Commission performed an intervention for a media so addicted to its own standpoint that it failed to report reality accurately. It was now time for the press to rehabilitate itself.

Hiring more African Americans in the newsrooms of "the white press," as recommended by the report, should, it would seem, have solved the problem of the improving coverage of African American life. Journalism is concerned with reporting about communities. Standpoint involves community. Thus, hiring more reporters from the black community adds a counterbalancing standpoint that allows the white press to report a more complete reality. During the last decade of the twentieth century, there were those who made the claim that the First Amendment provides a compelling rationale for newsroom diversity because "pluralism and diversity are its heart and soul."[19] Those who believe in the benefits of a diverse newsroom maintain that because America's future is a pluralistic one, newspapers' futures must be as well.[20]

However, at the start of the twenty-first century, the percentage of African Americans working at mainstream newspapers decreased slightly in 2000–2001.[21] According to the annual report released by the American Society of Newspaper Editors in 2001, African Americans made up 5 percent of journalists at newspapers in 2000, down .07 percent from the previous year.[22] This decline in African American percentage numbers was the first in twenty-three years.[23] Though the ASNE's 2008 report stated that the percentage of minority journalists working at daily newspapers rose slightly in 2007, from 13.43 percent to 13.52 percent, it still lags behind the percentage of minorities in the U.S. population, which is about 34 percent according to the U.S. Census Bureau.[24] After holding steady in 2001 and 2002, the number of minorities in newsrooms has increased every year since, from sixty-six hundred in 2001 to seventy-one hundred in 2008.[25] The increase in minority percentage numbers, however, comes amid a decrease in the number of journalists overall. In 2007 the industry lost twenty-four hundred jobs.[26] As the industry continues to shrink, there are growing concerns that newspapers may not remain truly committed to diversity.

However, there are those who wonder whether pursuing diversity actually helps to make journalism better. In his book *Coloring the News: How Political Correctness Has Corrupted American Journalism*, William McGowan states that even though newsroom diversity efforts are "a worthy, overdue and historically necessary" enterprise, they have run off the rails in their implementation.[27] He maintains that the pursuit of racial and gender diversity in the newsroom has not been conducive to dependable news coverage of controversial subjects involving race, politics, and class. Neither, he claims, has it been good for the nation as a whole, especially at this pivotal moment in our development as a multicultural society, when the demographic and cultural changes transforming our nation call for all the information that the "marketplace of ideas" can provide to help citizens make important democratic choices.

Furthermore, there are those who question the assumption that minority journalists can help newspapers relate to minority readers or do a better job of covering minority issues. They claim that minority journalists are trained in much the same way as nonminority journalists, sharing similar views about the importance of media roles, and as such can be assumed to have the same values.[28]

Though diversity naysayers are correct to be concerned about the ways in which diversity is achieved in the newsroom, their concerns about the effect of diversity on newsgathering are misplaced. Instead of criticizing the addition of men and women of color to newsrooms, which seems to be the subtext of their argument, they should consider the idea that reporters from diverse backgrounds might possibly allow consumers of journalism products—whether in print, broadcast, or online forms—to be exposed to different parts of the journalistic truth. More than that, they should also consider that even having the same journalism reported by someone of a different race or gender from an ethnic group is significant because it forces everyone to have to come to grips with the fact that competence and ability are not solely the providence of white men and women, which is ultimately the reason behind having diverse newsrooms.

Truth, Objectivity, and Autobiography

The problem stems, perhaps, from the lack of understanding of the socially constructed nature of truth and, as a result, of news. Lives lived in connection with other lives contribute to the construction of truth. It is because of this that analyzing and understanding the experiences of journalists from racial and ethnic minorities who have written about their work in the newsroom within the context of autobiography can and should be a site for academic examination. A study of African American journalism autobiographies will add to our understanding of the problems members of other underrepresented groups face in the workplace, whether as journalists or in other professions. Studying journalism autobiographies will also serve to illuminate how "truth" is reported from differing perspectives. The best way to engage in this exploration is by examining the life stories written by journalists of color, and specifically how they describe their newsroom experiences.

The literary merit of the autobiographies of journalists is best described by Howard Good, who posits:

> [Autobiographies] reveal . . . what a journalist is and how a journalist thinks and where a journalist goes, and they are novels, or like novels, because they imaginatively transform it, give it a coherence that was not there before. The autobiographer is no less a creative artist than the novelist. He makes his life a work of art.[29]

The autobiographer, then, makes art out of his or her life story by giving it the form of a narrative. For the journalist, the narrative form has a natural attraction for a person who has spent a career telling the stories of others. But there is a disadvantage to this. Margo Perkins notes that "any attempt to connect, and thereby interpret the meaning of, experiences from our past implicates us in a narrative process. This narrative process involves selecting or privileging some events at the expense of others. Ultimately, how we order or make meaning of past experience is determined by our own epistemological orientation," our own ways of being and creating knowledge.[30] It would seem that for a journalist, an autobiography is a site of conflict between the form's narrative demands and the profession's quixotic pursuit of objectivity.

It is not entirely inaccurate to describe the journalistic pursuit of objectivity as a quixotic quest. Objectivity is a concept whose existence needs to be explained as opposed to assumed. Michael Schudson states, "The belief in objectivity is a faith in 'facts,' a distrust of 'values,' and a commitment to their segregation."[31] Objectivity means more than collecting the facts; it means separating facts from values and developing a method by which to achieve this separation. The pursuit of objectivity in journalism is a recent one, according to Schudson; only in the years after World War I did it become an important value in American journalism.

Before World War I, journalists did not subscribe to the idea that facts and values could be separated. They were confident in their ability to find the truth and report it. During the 1920s, however, journalists' faith in facts was upset by World War I and the use of propaganda. Editors were becoming more aware of the use of propaganda and press agents' role in manipulating facts.[32] Schudson maintains that objectivity was pursued as a "scientific" solution to the fact that reporters were losing faith in journalism as fact finding.[33] Walter Lippmann and others started to call for ways in which the journalist could be free of his or her biases—to strive for a type of reporting of reality not subject to emotional influence—in reporting the news.[34] Eventually, the concept of objectivity as envisioned by Lippmann transformed into a "set of practices or conventions that the professional journalist is trained to follow."[35]

David T. Z. Mindich offers a different perspective on the history of journalistic objectivity as practice. He views objectivity as an assemblage of connected practices that have separate origins. With this in mind, he identifies five components that comprise journalistic objectivity: detachment, nonpartisanship, the inverted pyramid structure, facticity, and balance.[36] According to Mindich, detachment as a practice arose as a reaction to the violence of the 1830s.[37] For nonpartisanship he identifies a range of positions, from James Gordon Bennett's centrism, William Lloyd Garrison's "antipartisan" stance, to Frederick Douglass's "activist" nonpartisanism.[38] The inverted pyramid structure in journalism—telling a story from end to beginning, from biggest point to smaller ones—is now standard. According to Mindich, this practice has its origins in the Civil War—as an innovation not from a news organization, but from Edwin Stanton and the War Department, whose dispatches were printed by most newspapers.[39] A form such as the inverted pyramid structure that conceals the processing of information and makes it seem natural has ominous implications that should be guarded against. Mindich maintains that "[a]s modern journalists seek truth in a balance of authoritative sound bites and quotes, they should keep in mind how information, when cleverly managed and manipulated, may give little more than the government's side of the story."[40]

Facticity was part of the scientific approach that was shared by the medical and journalism establishments that arose during the middle of the nineteenth century. During this time, "[m]edicine, art, literature, the social sciences, and journalism rejected a religious paradigm in favor of a scientific one," according to Mindich.[41]

The last decade of the nineteenth century, Mindich maintains, can be considered the first one in which objectivity was a recognized practice in journalism, but that decade was also the last in which the concept "goes basically unquestioned."[42] Mindich asserts that during the 1890s, the "false balance" objectivity created—as practiced through nonpartisanship, the use of the inverted pyramid style, and facticity—provide a context for reporters to accurately report on lynching.[43] He presents Ida B. Wells's crusade against lynching and against the failure of newspapers to fully report on the nature of lynching as a critique of the failure of objectivity. In her crusade, Wells was by no means an objective reporter, but, Mindich states, "perhaps some reporters ought not be."[44]

In its strictest usage, the term "objectivity" suggests that journalism means to be "so utterly disinterested as to be transparent."[45] In essence, reporting on an issue becomes virtually the issue itself, uncensored, unfiltered by the mind of the reporter.[46] But, as Fuller maintains, this is impossible: "No one has ever achieved objective journalism, and no one ever could. The bias of the observer always enters the picture, if not coloring the details, at least guiding the choice of them."[47] A reporter may be able to recognize his or her biases and try to adjust for them, but that transforms the reporting process and the product of that process into a work that is highly subjective. Moreover, it requires an almost machine-like mental state that is difficult to achieve. Acknowledging this failing of objectivity as a journalistic principle would seem to validate the value of a diverse newsroom. If there are people with diverse backgrounds reporting the truth from various perspectives—even perspectives that might possibly overlap with the perspectives of people in the main-stream—then a more complete version of the truth emerges, composed of multiple limited subjectivities. These subjectivities are limited only by the fact that people's lived experiences differ.

Memory and Objectivity

If, for the journalist, objectivity is as mythical as a unicorn and truth is fluid and contested, then it is through facts and memory that reporters, like other writers, must arrive at the truth. Memory, at once shaped by and conjoined with experience, serves as the source text for journalists and autobiographers. Reporters often rely on the memories of sources in their reporting. Autobiographers rely on the memory of their own experiences in presenting their life stories.

However, as a concept, "memory" is itself as illusory and problematic as "truth" or "objectivity." The memory of the autobiographer is one that "consists of material learned, not by heart, but by soul, by a com-plicated pattern of psychological self-deceptions and constructions."[48] This suggests that the autobiographer reconstructs him- or herself from the soul outward. Truth filters through emotion and memory, leaving readers with an examined life that privileges subjective remembrances of experience. This presents a problematic situation because readers want to believe that what they read is the "whole truth."

But subjective remembrances are less problematic than they seem, because the truth will eventually rise from what has been written. Peter Ives maintains that autobiographical writers do not experience or write about events as they actually happened; instead, they write about them as the writers themselves "happened." That is, autobiographical writers describe events in their works that emerge from an incomplete, albeit immediate, set of situations. Still, this does not pose a problem because, he states, between a writer's memory and reality "are the shadows from which the truth will ultimately reassert itself."[49] The autobiographer cannot help but write the truth: The truth will emerge because it will seep in to what the writer creates, at least as far as the reader is concerned.

Moreover, there is a necessity for the type of memory connected to experience:

> Involuntary memory—what is called up from deep emotional experience and of its own accord—is immensely valuable to writers of any genre. It is far more complicated than fact—the bus schedules of voluntary memory. It is where the heart and soul of our past resides.[50]

Thus, what emerges in autobiography comes from the "heart and soul" of the past, and, as a result, is the truth. Or it is something close enough to the truth that readers who want, in Peter M. Ives's terms, "to be told a story" can accept it as truth.[51] In the end, both writer and reader collaborate in creating the "truth" of the story because, as Kenneth Mostern writes, "the autobiographer may be perfectly aware that language cannot guarantee the truth of anything, and yet use the trope of autobiography specifically because in the legal and political community they inhabit, they choose to document their references."[52] Autobiography becomes a tool through which the writer presents a story, and because the reader enters the autobiographical world expecting what is written about a life to be true, it is accepted as truth.

In the end, Mostern maintains, truth emerges in autobiography because "there are (artistic, cultural, political) reasons for telling a publicly comprehensible truth."[53] The autobiographer feels a sense of responsibility to present the truth. Jerome Bruner states that the autobiographical writer cannot reflect on the self without reflecting upon the environment he or she inhabits.[54] However, "one's reflections on both one's self and one's world cannot be one's own alone: you and your version of your world must be public, recognizable enough to be negotiable in the 'conversation of lives.'"[55] The reflections in an autobiography must communicate to their readers because they are representative.[56]

Ultimately, truth and memory are like marble and clay. Truth, like marble, is solid, and we can chisel away at it. If a writer is skilled enough, he or she can shape it into statues or sculptures without getting away from Fern Kupfer's idea of literal truth—something akin to the journalistic goal of reporting what actually happened. Memory, in contrast, is like clay; it has a malleability that allows it to be shaped into different forms. Clay can be shaped into pottery, but, like truth, it can be shaped into sculpture as well. Memory is akin to the aesthetic or artistic truth that Kupfer describes. Within the aesthetic truth, there exist three levels of "lying"—of shaping the truth. Two levels allow writers to shape the truth but stay within the bounds of reality—a retouching or selective omission of details, if you will. The third, "the gift of perhaps," is a kind of conjecture that allows writers to fill the spaces of memory with scenes created from whole cloth—a counterfeiting of the truth.[57] The place of truth and memory in autobiography is a contested, conflicted one, but it is never beyond exploration. The analyses that follow explore the way in which truth and memory can bring to life, in the autobiographical form, a bold statement about the complexities of being black in America.

Notes

1. U.S. Census Bureau, "An Older and More Diverse Nation by Midcentury," press release, August 14, 2008.

2. U.S. Census Bureau, "An Older and More Diverse Nation by Midcentury."

3. Bill Kovach and Tom Rosenstiel, *The Elements of Journalism: What Newspeople Should Know and the Public Should Expect* (New York: Crown, 2001), 42.

4. Kovach and Rosenstiel, *The Elements of Journalism*, 41.

5. Jack Fuller, *News Values: Ideas for an Information Age* (Chicago: University of Chicago Press, 1996), 2.

6. Fuller, *News Values*, 4.

7. Fuller, *News Values*, 4.

8. Lee Hubbard, "Mainstream Newspapers Fade to White," May 1, 2001, http://lists.topica.com/lists/TheBlackList/read/message.html?sort=t&mid=130 3992223.

9. Pamela Newkirk, *Within the Veil: Black Journalists, White Media* (New York: New York University Press, 2000), 36.

10. Of course, the path of African American journalists to the newsrooms of the white mainstream did not occur simply as a two-step process of historical events—the founding of *Freedom's Journal* in 1827 and the release of the Kerner Commission Report in 1968. The growth and development of the black press throughout the nineteenth and twentieth centuries also played an essential role, but an analysis of that development is outside the focus of this study.

11. *Report of the National Advisory Commission on Civil Disorders* (New York: Bantam Books, 1968), 1.

12. *National Advisory Commission on Civil Disorders*, 363.

13. *National Advisory Commission on Civil Disorders.*

14. *National Advisory Commission on Civil Disorders*, 371.

15. *National Advisory Commission on Civil Disorders*, 365.

16. *National Advisory Commission on Civil Disorders*, 365.

17. Carolyn Martindale, *The White Press and Black America*, Contributions in Afro-American and African Studies, No. 97 (Westport, CT: Greenwood, 1986), 54.

18. *Report of the National Advisory Commission on Civil Disorders* (New York: Bantam, 1968), 366.

19. Donna Allen, "Women, Minorities & Freedom of the Press," *Newspaper Research Journal* 11 (1990), 10–17.

20. David Lawrence, "Broken Ladders, Revolving Doors: The Need for Pluralism in the Newsroom," *Newspaper Research Journal* 11 (1990).

21. Hubbard, "Mainstream Newspapers Fade to White."

22. ASNE, "2001 ASNE Census Finds Newsrooms Less Diverse: Increased Hiring of Minorities Blunted by Departure Rate," press release, April 3, 2001, www.asne.org/kiosk/diversity/2001Survey/2001CensusReport.htm.

23. ASNE, "2001 ASNE Census Finds Newsrooms Less Diverse: Increased Hiring of Minorities Blunted by Departure Rate."

24. ASNE, "Newsroom Employment Census," April 12, 2005, www.asne.org/index.cfm?id=5646.

25. ASNE, "Newsroom Employment Census."

26. ASNE, "Newsroom Employment Census."

27. William McGowan, *Coloring the News: How Crusading for Diversity Has Corrupted American Journalism* (San Francisco: Encounter Books, 2001), 7.

28. George Sylvie and Patricia Dennis Witherspoon, *Time, Change and the American Newspaper*, Lea's Communication Series (Mahwah, NJ: Lawrence Erlbaum Associates, 2002).

29. Howard Good, *The Journalist as Autobiographer* (Metuchen, NJ: Scarecrow Press, 1993), 3.

30. Margo V. Perkins, *Autobiography as Activism: Three Black Women of the Sixties* (Jackson: University Press of Mississippi, 2000), 41–42.

31. Michael Schudson, *Discovering the News* (New York: BasicBooks, 1978), 6.

32. Kovach and Rosenstiel, *The Elements of Journalism*, 73.

33. Schudson, *Discovering the News*, 6.

34. Kovach and Rosenstiel, *The Elements of Journalism*, 73.

35. David Croteau and William Hoynes, *Media/Society: Industries, Images, and Audiences*, 3rd ed. (Thousand Oaks, CA: Pine Forge, 2003), 133.

36. David T. Z. Mindich, *Just the Facts: How "Objectivity" Came to Define American Journalism* (New York: New York University Press, 1998).

37. Mindich, *Just the Facts*, 39.

38. Mindich, *Just the Facts*, 41–63.

39. Mindich, *Just the Facts*, 64–94.

40. Mindich, *Just the Facts*, 93.

41. Mindich, *Just the Facts*, 95.

42. Mindich, *Just the Facts*, 114.

43. Mindich, *Just the Facts*, 137.

44. Mindich, *Just the Facts*, 137.

45. Fuller, *News Values*, 14.

46. Fuller, *News Values*.

47. Fuller, *News Values*, 14.

48. Timothy Dow Adams, *Telling Lies in Modern American Autobiography* (Chapel Hill: University of North Carolina Press, 1990), 169.

49. Peter M. Ives, "The Whole Truth," in *The Fourth Genre: Contemporary Writers of/on Creative Nonfiction*, ed. Robert L. Root and Michael Steinberg (New York: Longman, 2002), 275.

50. Patricia Hampl, "Memory and Imagination," in *The Fourth Genre: Contemporary Writers of/on Creative Nonfiction*, ed. Michael Steinberg (New York: Longman, 2002), 273.

51. Ives, "The Whole Truth," 271.

52. Kenneth Mostern, *Autobiography and Black Identity Politics: Racialization in Twentieth-Century America*, Cultural Margins, no. 7 (New York: Cambridge University Press, 1999), 38.

53. Mostern, *Autobiography and Black Identity Politics*, 38.

54. Jerome Bruner, "The Autobiographical Process," in *The Culture of Autobiography: Constructions of Self-Representation*, ed. Robert Folkenflik, Irvine Studies in the Humanities (Stanford, CA: Stanford University Press, 1993), 43.

55. Bruner, "The Autobiographical Process," 43.

56. Bruner, "The Autobiographical Process," 43.

57. Fern Kupfer, "Everything but the Truth?" in *The Fourth Genre: Contemporary Writers of/on Creative Nonfiction*, ed. Robert L. Root and Michael Steinberg (New York: Longman, 2002), 293.

2

Form, Function and the Public Sphere in Jill Nelson's *Volunteer Slavery*

S TRIVING FOR DIVERSE NEWSROOMS has led to unforeseen issues for black journalists. A study by Ted Pease and Guido H. Stempel, conducted twenty-two years after the Kerner Commission Report, painted a bleak picture for managers of color in the newsroom. It stated that many of them did not get the same kind of consideration as their white colleagues, a lack of fair treatment that "seems in some cases accidental—or at least unconscious—but often racial," according to the survey respondents.[1] Carol M. Liebler's study of newsroom autonomy found that female journalists believe they have as much autonomy as male journalists, but minority journalists perceive themselves as having slightly less.[2] But a study by Richard Gross, Patricia A. Curtin, and Glen T. Cameron consisting of interviews with seventy-six *Los Angeles Times* newsroom employees found that the paper's program to enhance diversity in its content and newsroom staff, coupled with an increase in profits through broader circulation in ethnic communities, strengthened the paper.[3]

There exists a unique African American viewpoint that has developed out of the special sociohistorical position of black people in the United States—the aforementioned "double consciousness" of W. E. B. Du Bois. This suggests a different conception, perhaps, of journalistic values such as objectivity that conflicts with the nature of the newsroom culture.

One of the main purposes of this discussion is to uncover the roles memoirs play within the public sphere in helping us understand the particular role of the African American journalist.

The public sphere is a *social* sphere. Within it, all interactions among its members are social ones, resulting in the creation of values and knowledge that the members share with each other. For good or ill, there is a shared sense of what is "natural," and what is "common-sense"—a particularized understanding of the social world that suggests that individuals accept a particular ideology about social relations within that sphere. The existence of parallel public/social spheres suggests the possibility of an infinite number of such spheres, each with its own set of commonsense assumptions but contained within the dominant public sphere.

For members of those parallel public spheres, autobiography serves as a way of questioning the assumptions in the dominant public sphere by challenging dominant commonplace assumptions about individual members of the marginalized public spheres. Autobiographies present evidence of how lives are *effected* and *affected* by interactions with others, both within the particular public spheres to which they belong and outside of those spheres. Multiple interactions take place in a single life, and thus the autobiographer is the chronicler not of a single life story, but of the story of the interactions among many lives. "We tend to think of autobiography as literature of the first person," Paul John Eakin states, "but the subject of autobiography to which the pronoun 'I' refers is neither singular nor first, and we do well to demystify its claims."[4]

So, to analyze an autobiography written by a member of a marginalized public sphere is to uncover and define how that life has been shaped by its interactions with members of other public spheres. As a result, the life story of one person explicates other people's experiences and issues of concern. Moreover, if the personal is the political, autobiographical texts exist as more than literary documents. They are documents imbued with political power; the authors speak on behalf of a collective. They are, in a general sense, manifestos, documents that are, as Janet Lyon says, "constitutive of the public sphere to the degree that it persistently registers the contradictions within modern political life."[5] They document the disconnect between a society's ideals and its practice.

John Hartley claims that modern political life—political modernity—has its genesis in the transfer of power from absolute monarchs to the people in the form of representative democracy.[6] One of the hallmarks of this power transfer is the promise of individual freedom coexisting with collective action. But this is sometimes a false promise; one of the downsides of modernity is the existence of the exploitation and the marginalization of members of the public sphere:

> For while modernity offers ideological assurances of autonomy and individualism within collectivity, it also and at the same time draws on the deferral of these promises. The manifesto records just this breach between modernity's promissory notes and their payment.[7]

The purpose of the manifesto, then, is to hold those in power accountable for abuses of their power. And no matter who the author is and no matter what the subject of the manifesto is, it is "understood as the testimony of a historical present tense spoken in the impassioned voices of its participants."[8] A manifesto stakes out a position on an issue, refusing to engage in dialogue or discussion. It is a confrontational document that is "univocal, unilateral, single-minded" and exists to convey "resolute oppositionality and indulges no tolerance for the fainthearted."[9] Anyone who writes a manifesto places him- or herself in the participatory circle of the struggle against the forces of oppression and marginalization. A manifesto is part of an "overdetermined history of modernity that involves the emergence of public spheres and the rise of the modern state," and they are spawned at the "cloverleafs of class war, gender politics, ethnic identification, and national struggle."[10] At these intersections, manifestos proliferate, and the manifesto author appropriates the role of statesman, warrior, even demagogue, as necessary to confront the sovereignty of the oppressor. Autobiography provides a means of accomplishing this task.

Autobiographical Manifestos Revisited

Sidonie Smith describes a manifesto as "a proof, a piece of evidence, a public declaration or proclamation . . . for the purpose of announcing past actions and explaining the reasons or motives for actions announced as forthcoming."[11] It is from this definition that she extracts the six characteristics used to define the autobiographical manifesto that are the focus of this study. In Smith's view, however, the autobiographical manifesto is a type of "anti-autobiographical form"—part of a genre that consists of "autobiographical but eclectically 'errant' and culturally disruptive writing practices."[12] The suggestion here is that the autobiographical manifesto does not necessarily follow the form or structure typical of what may be considered an "autobiography"—lived experiences told in the form of narrative prose. An autobiographical manifesto may depart radically from that structure.

But structure is also important to the manifesto, autobiographical or not. As defined by Smith, Lyon, and others, the manifesto has characteristics that define its structure. Even so, these characteristics do not place limitations on what a manifesto can be; they only describe, in general, what has been. But, if employed correctly, those characteristics may be radical enough to create documents that effectively critique society and suggest ways to change it. The discussion of the autobiographies in the succeeding analyses will explore how using the form of the autobiographical narrative allows members of marginalized publics to produce autobiographical works that function effectively as autobiographical manifestos.

Jill Nelson and the Confrontation of Sovereignty

As we have already discussed, the autobiographical manifesto allows its subject to assert itself in the locale of the "universal subject." However, Smith maintains that the universal subject is a place that "consolidates sovereignty through exclusionary practices. These practices figure 'others' as 'not-an-individualized-'I,'" persons whose humanity is opaque, and whose membership in the human community is negated by relegation to . . . a chaotic, disorganized and anonymous collectivity."[13] Autobiographical manifestos come from people who, having been assigned to anonymous collectivity, "vigorously reject the sovereignty of this specular *ancien régime* and the dominance of the universal subject."[14] In order to assert its own identity, the autobiographical subject subordinates the "universal subject," rendering it empty. Manifestos allow the autobiographical subject to confront the "ghost of the identity assigned . . . by the old sovereign subject . . . a fixed object position representing culturally intelligible and authorized performances of identity."[15] Such "performances" of identity include gender and ethnicity, but the autobiographical manifesto allows the subjects to redefine those identities in their own standpoint-specific ways.

In autobiographical manifestos, then, subjects either appropriate or contest sovereignty. That is, subjects appropriate a space in the central standpoint from which to report their experiences, and in so doing create their own identities, ignoring the exclusionary politics that have allowed the universal subject to assert its primacy; or they contest sovereignty by rejecting the idea of the universal subject, asserting that their individual identity is more valid than their consignment to an anonymous collectivity. But let us now move from discussions of the principles in the abstract to examining the concept at work in Jill Nelson's memoir.

Nelson's 1993 memoir, *Volunteer Slavery: My Authentic Negro Experience*, documents her experiences as the first black female writer at the *Washington Post* Sunday magazine. As she chronicles her lack of power in the newsroom, she also examines her ongoing struggle to define herself as a member of upper-middle-class black society, and to define her own terms of success outside of the possibilities her upbringing suggests. Because she is an African American female, Nelson inhabits both racialized and gendered public spheres. As a result, her autobiography does double duty as a document that speaks for both marginalized publics. There is much to be gained from its examination because, as Joanne Braxton states, studying African American women's participation in autobiographical writing can reveal a great deal about how the lived experience of racial and sexual difference may influence the development of identity.[16]

In that regard, to discuss appropriation/contestation of sovereignty in *Volunteer Slavery*, means interrogating how *Volunteer Slavery* functions as an autobiographical manifesto that depicts Nelson's search for "authentic Negro experiences" in the professional, personal, and family dimensions. The "double consciousness" described by Du Bois forms part of her identity, but her ultimate quest is for a single "authentic" self who can be a good journalist/employee, good friend/lover, and good daughter/sister without sacrificing any part of who she is.

Nelson is aware of the advantages she had growing up as a member of the black middle class, but in order to appropriate sovereignty for her single "authentic" self, Nelson contests the sovereignty of the double-consciousness paradigm in her family life. *Volunteer Slavery* opens *in medias res*, with Nelson in the middle of her *Washington Post* job interview. She is "tired of being on," tired of the interview performance she has to engage in when she knows the true reason for her interest in the *Post* job: "[T]he notion of coming to work at the *Washington Post* is mostly about money, but that's a black thing, which [white] people would never understand."[17] Her interview situation is typical of one any prospective employee, black or white, might face in that she has to be "on" for her prospective employers. But even as she does this, she also divests herself of any pretense of double consciousness. Her pursuit of the job is situated in blackness; blackness, for her, is not about the status that comes from being a reporter at the *Post*. It is about monetary security—for her, the only type of power that is transferable across public spheres.

Her interview with *Post* executive editor Ben Bradlee, as presented by Nelson, shows her having to confront a white person's possible expectations about what constitutes black life. When Bradlee says, "Tell me something about yourself," Nelson begins to think about a song—specifically, the Temptations' "Papa Was a Rollin' Stone," which she feels may incorrectly define "the authentic Negro experience" for white people.[18] She counters that idea with the truth: Her family was "solidly upper-middle-class." In addition, she writes that "[t]he day of the glorification of the stereotypical poor, pathological Negro is over. Just like the South, it is time for the black bourgeoisie to rise again. I am a foot soldier in that Army."[19] She refuses to accept the idea that she must somehow portray herself as having risen from a deprived background in order to make her interviewer feel more comfortable with her. She regales Bradlee with tales of her upper-middle-class upbringing—of prep schools and summers spent among the black bourgeoisie. This allows her to transcend the dividing line of race, at least for a time, into the dividing line of class. Not only is this truer to her upbringing, it makes Bradlee more comfortable with her. She becomes merely a middle-class person:

> Our eyes meet, our chuckle ends, and I know I'm over. The job is mine. Simply by evoking residence on Martha's Vineyard, I have separated wheat from chaff, belongers from aspirers, rebellious chip-on-the-shoulder Negroes from middle-class, responsible ones.
>
> Vanquished is the leftist ghost of my years writing for the *Village Voice*. Gone are the fears he might have had about my fitting in after a life as a freelance writer, an advocacy journalist, a free black. By dint of summers spent on Martha's Vineyard, I am, in his eyes, safe. I may be the darker sister, but I'm still a sister. I will fit into the *Washington Post* family.[20]

Nelson believes that she will be able to "fit in" at the *Post* based on the assumption of a shared class standpoint based on class. She believes that, for Bradlee, this may negate any negative assumptions that come from dealing with matters of race. However, when she begins working at the *Post*, she is marginalized and basically ignored from the outset, particularly by Jay Lovinger, the editor who so eagerly participated in her recruitment—"as if it is enough that I am merely there and I don't have to worry about *doing* anything."[21] Moreover, she's given an editorial position—that of "D.C. assignments editor"—only to find that she has no power to assign stories. Nelson later discovers that in 1980 the newspaper had entered a consent decree with the Equal Employment Opportunity Commission that mandated the paper make a "good-faith effort" to hire more women.

Throughout *Volunteer Slavery*, Nelson stresses the idea of "authenticity"—of that which is real. But any "authentic" experience she has is contained in, and informed by, a black standpoint that is subsumed within the dominant standpoint. So her quest for "authentic Negro experiences" is ultimately a quest for a space in which black people's experiences are valued and respected. Throughout the book, Nelson presents episodes that show that what is "real" for her as a black person has no value to white editors and reporters. For example, when she is shown the first issue of the *Post*'s magazine, she encounters the disconnect between blacks and whites: Its cover features a photograph of "a young black man, printed in dark browns and grays, fading first into shadow, then into black" for a story titled "Murder, Drugs, and the Rap Star."[22] She continues, "The man looks threatening, furtive, hostile, and guilty: Richard Wright's fictional Bigger Thomas, who chopped up a white girl and stuffed her in the furnace, made real and transposed to the 1980s. The ultimate nightmare Negro."[23] When asked by her editor, a white woman, what she thinks of the cover, Nelson refrains from expressing her true feelings in the newsroom:

What I want to say is "I think this looks horrible. It plays into white folk's stereotypes of young black men as inherently dangerous and rap music as fomenting racist insurrection. Plus the photograph is ugly, it's too dark and evil looking. Is this really going to be the first issue of the magazine so many black folks in this city have so eagerly awaited? This is not going to go over. . . ."[24]

But she tempers her response. "I choose my words carefully," she writes. "I don't want to sound the way the brother looks on the cover: hostile, alienated, potentially dangerous."[25] She merely says, "I don't love it," a reply Nelson says makes her "both diplomat and chicken-shit."[26] She declines to state her true feelings about the cover for fear of alienating herself from her new coworkers. She subordinates the needs of the black public sphere—to be understood as more than what the magazine cover signifies—to those of the dominant public sphere in which she works. Nelson realizes the penalty she will face in the black community. When she asks her editor if she has talked to the person responsible for the cover, the editor dismisses the question. Nelson reflects on this:

> Easy for her. [The editor] may be a feminist-progressive type who's dated black men, but she ain't black. She can go to beaucoup anti-apartheid rallies, but she'll never be a race woman, never understand what it is to be compulsively, irrevocably, painfully responsible not only for herself, but for her race. By virtue of my skin color, I'm going to take the weight for this if the shit hits the fan. Black folks are going to look at me and ask, "Why didn't you do something?"[27]

Like other reporters from marginalized groups who work in the newsrooms of the mainstream press, Nelson carries with her the weight of expectations of all the members of the group. Whether or not she should carry this weight is not an issue. Nelson becomes the sole representative of a particular standpoint, in a contact zone that is the newsroom of the mainstream newspaper who hired her. It is not a neutral playing field. The fallout from this clash of standpoints is a series of protests that take place at the *Post* because of the "Murder, Drugs, and the Rap Star" story.

For Neslon, the fallout begins at home, when a friend calls to complain about a column written by the *Post's* Richard Cohen: "My phone starts ringing Saturday evening, a few hours after the home-delivery subscribers receive their 'throwaways': circulars, coupons, and cartoons. As it turns out, the magazine is soon to be the biggest throwaway of them all." The complaints continue into the night:

> Everyone who calls me is black. No one has anything positive to say. In their outrage, paranoia reigns. Just about everyone sees the publication

of the Cohen and Bradley articles in the first issue as a diabolical, pre-meditated racist attack on D.C.'s black community by the *Washington Post*. The consensus is that the newspaper commissioned and printed the two articles—both of which portray black youth (and by extension, some argue, the black community) as criminal—as an intentional and organized slap in the face.

It does not occur to them that the institution that is the *Washington Post* seldom devotes much thought to black people at all, and that the editors and managers aren't diabolical. They just screwed up.[28]

Nelson realizes that she should have been more aware of the paper's lack of concern for detail and lack of foresight when she received a call from one of her references, notifying her that the paper had just called them to get a reference for her—two weeks after she started the job. But what the episode really illustrates is that the editors—all of them white—"screwed up" because they did not consider the possibility that other standpoints might be valid. Moreover, Nelson's assertion that the editors and managers made mistakes in choosing stories for the magazine emanates from her own individual standpoint, one that is separate and distinct from that of the larger black community in Washington, D.C. It is her assessment of the editors' work. The black community—or at least those who called to complain about the magazine—sees a conspiratorial attempt to denigrate blacks. Nelson, on the other hand, sees merely professionals who made an error in judgment—one that cost the paper the respect of a black community that was already suspicious of it. But because she is a member of a marginalized group—and a member of a newsroom culture whose white members' understanding of black culture is limited by what Newkirk says is their failure to "fully explore the complexity of black life"[29]—Nelson inhabits a unique space from which she appropriates a kind of individual sovereignty. Within the pages of *Volunteer Slavery*, this particular type of sovereignty allows her to not only critique the actions of the managers and editors of the magazine, but the black community in Washington, D.C.:

> I've lived in Washington a few months, but it's clear that the black folks here take themselves extremely seriously. With the largest black middle-class population of any city in the country, they not only have a strong—and sometimes distorted—sense of their own importance, but the numbers to make a *lot* of noise.[30]

Nelson states that she is a "race woman," but she is also a journalist. The fact that she serves in these two capacities allows her to use autobiographical form to appropriate sovereignty in the manner that is required of the autobiographical manifesto. Appropriation means to take on for oneself, to act in the role of. To be a journalist is the act of appropriation, as one of the roles of the journalist is to report by acting as the eyes, ears, and voice of the citizens for whom they report. The role of the journalist of color is doubly so.

The Manifestation of Experience

The second of the constituent aspects of autobiographical manifestos is "[t]o bring to light, to make manifest"—that is, to bring issues into the "light of day."[31] Autobiographical manifestos expose issues that are confined to the outer edges of the public sphere. In doing so, they become sites in which accounts from the margins are significant because they are reports that can, as Nancy Hartsock maintains, show the falsity of the view of the world from the predominant standpoint and, as a result, can change the margins and the center.[32] Autobiographical manifestos, like manifestos in general, present the opportunity for transformative actions in the domain of the public sphere:

> Intent on bringing culturally marginalized experiences out from under the shadow of an undifferentiated otherness, the autobiographical manifesto anchors its narrative itinerary in the specificities and locales of time and space, the discursive surround, the material ground, the provenance of histories.[33]

Moreover, as John Sturrock states, "Autobiographers inevitably record details of contemporary life that are too small and too ordinary to have been found worth recording in any official source, as well as their own reactions and attitudes toward all manner of events."[34] Autobiographical manifestos present the small details along with the larger stories of those who inhabit the marginalized public spheres—and specific sociocultural locations. By doing this, autobiographical manifestos become places in which analyses of the intersections of the social, psychological, economic, and political forces of oppression—which Hartsock defines as part of standpoint epistemology—can take place.[35]

These intersections and confluences, and the issues that arise from the conflicts within them, are made manifest in the life narrative.

In *Volunteer Slavery*, the forces of oppression that come together in Nelson's life are centered along the fault lines of race, class, and gender, but it is the racial fault line that forms the predominant standpoint from which Nelson views the world. Not only does she have to cope with the kind of marginalization that blacks face in the public sphere at the hands of white people, she also has to be aware of intra-racial oppression and prejudice centered around whites' expectations of who blacks should be and the impact of those expectations on black peoples' interactions with each other. This is evidenced by her description of her close friendship with a writer and editor at the *Village Voice*:

> Initially, we greeted each other with suspicion. Middle-class black folks, especially those with straight or psuedo-straight hair who are nearer light-skinned than dark, tend to grow up feeling we have something to prove—not just to white folks but to just about everyone, including each other. We greet one another with skepticism, treating each other as potential Euro-centric sell-outs . . . until proven otherwise. We scrutinize each other for signs that we are trading on our color or class to get over. We examine each other's attitudes about race and self through our own internal microscopes of fear and self-doubt, looking for indications that we have allowed our educational and material success to distance us from "the people."[36]

But the main issue Nelson brings into the light of day is how the staff and management who work for the *Post* react to the black community's protests after the publication of the "Rap Star" issue. Nelson says that "[i]n spite of the incessantly ringing phones and the grumblings of other staff members," the *Post*'s staff underestimated the anger of D.C.'s black residents.[37] They assumed the black community's anger would subside during the week after the issue's publication. It does not; if anything, it grows more intense. Nelson describes the nature of the black community's reaction to the "Rap Star" issue:

> The premiere issue quickly becomes grist for the local talk shows. . . . A coalition of forty-seven community organizations, including the Washington Urban league and the Archdiocese of Washington, forms the Washington Post Magazine Recall Committee. . . . The coalition demands that the *Post* suspend publication of the magazine and initiate talks about

what the coalition sees as ongoing negative depictions of the black community in the newspaper. Once it becomes organized and articulated, the anger of the black community becomes news.[38]

But in order to make this more than just a description of the reactions of a group—in order to bring to light the major issues at hand—Nelson must provide a contrasting insight. By doing this, she creates meaning, making salient the issues that concern the community. For Nelson, the making of meaning comes in the form of her discussion of the reaction of most of the white members of the *Post* staff to the protests. She writes:

> When [editor Jay] Lovinger isn't in meetings or at home passing kidney stones, he calls us together to tell us that he stands by the story and is confident the brouhaha will soon blow over. John Ed Bradley [the writer of the "Murder, Drugs, and the Rap Star" story] lounges around the office with red eyes, looking persecuted. My colleagues pat him on the back, squeeze his arm, make jokes, offer sympathy, as if somehow it is the black community that has done him wrong—conveniently ignoring management's monumental fuck-up.[39]

She continues by stating that she envies "their arrogance, their inherent belief in the efficacy of whatever they're doing, the smugness that comes from years of simply being Caucasian and, for the really fortunate, having a penis."[40] Because they operate from the privileged standpoints of whiteness and maleness, the *Post* staffers are unable or unwilling to consider that they may have erred in the choosing of the stories for the revamped magazine. Instead of considering the idea that they may have made a mistake in judgment, they simply cast the black protesters in the role of persecutors of the innocent. The memoir that acts as an autobiographical manifesto confronts the myopia that is part of privileged standpoints.

Autobiographical manifestos are rooted in the distinguishing attributes and places of time and space and the origins of histories. Nelson connects her work experiences to specific incidents in her life that are particularly revelatory. Most are incidents that involve family, particularly her father. For instance, when she decides to take the job at the *Post*, she has a dream—"more of a memory than a dream," she says—about her father in which he stresses the importance of being "Number one! Not two! Number one!"[41] In Nelson's memory-dream, her father is adamant that twelve-year-old Jill and her siblings strive for success:

> "You kids have got to be, not number two," he roars, his dark face turning darker from the effort to communicate. He holds up his index and middle fingers. "But number—" here, he pauses dramatically, a preacher going for revelation, his four children a rapt congregation, my mother a smitten church sister. "Number one!"[42]

But his exhortation is not without its irony. Nelson writes that while he makes his statement, her father slowly draws back the index finger, leaving only the middle finger. "That finger seemed to grow, thicken and harden, thrust up and at us, a phallic symbol to spur us . . . on to greatness, to number oneness," she writes.[43] Later she states that it was not until after her parents separated that she realized what the middle-finger gesture meant in everyday use, and that her father obviously knew the meaning. But, she says, she still does not know what message he was trying to impart to his children: "Were we to become number one and go out and intentionally fuck the world? If we didn't, would life fuck us? Was he intentionally trying sending his children a mixed message? If so, what was he trying to say?"[44] This memory-dream underlies the quest Nelson's autobiography defines in its pages. Her search for the "authentic Negro experience" is actually a quest for what it means to be "number one" as defined by her father's cryptic command and hand gesture. It is the quest for a level of success that marks its achiever as defiant, confident, and unashamed.

In the final analysis, what Nelson exposes to the light of day are the ways in which the standpoints of members of marginalized groups fail to be taken into account in the newsroom setting. The newsroom is the larger society in microcosm, reflecting its norm—a norm in which, according to Jannette Dates and Edward Pease, "the perspectives of white, mainstream men generally create the lenses through which America . . . views race, and itself."[45] The result is that other perspectives, other possibilities for seeing the world, are warped—or, even worse, left unexamined.

Public Announcement and Public Performance

In defining the ability "to announce publicly" as characteristic of auto-biographical manifestos, Smith states that, in general, all autobiographical writing is "a gesture toward publicity, displaying before an imper-sonal public an individual's interpretation of experience."[46] In African American autobiography, in particular, the "gesture toward publicity" is part of a long-standing tradition of written political expression. According to Kenneth Mostern, "the tradition of African-American writing is thus one in which political commentary necessitates, invites, and assumes autobiography as its rhetorical form."[47] As a result, much African American autobiographical writing can be assumed to be public announcement and/or performance of some sort.

Smith lists the performative aspect of the autobiographical manifesto as a separate characteristic. She maintains that the manifesto is "expressly a public performance" that "revels in the energetic display of a new kind of subject."[48] However, with African American autobiography, the announcement and performance facets are so closely intertwined in the tradition of African American writing that they can be analyzed together. The autobiographies written by journalists used in this study have their origins in the African American literary tradition. As a result, I will examine the announcement and performance facets together. The questions to consider here are: *What is being announced/performed?* and *What is the form of the announcement/performance?* That is, *how is the announcement/performance being done?*

I am assuming here that the performer is the subject of the autobiographical manifesto, so there is no need to answer the question of who is performing the announcment. However, in answering the first question, we need to consider the idea that such content is directly related to the impulse that drives the writer of the text. Smith states that "[t]he very impetus for contemporary autobiographical manifestos . . . lies in the recognition of a vexed relationship between what too easily becomes the binary opposition between the political and the personal."[49] The impact of the political on the personal and the conflict that arises from it drives the writing of an autobiographical manifesto.

For the writer of the autobiographical manifesto, the binary opposition between what is personal and what is political is a conflicted relationship for which there is no easy division; there is no obvious boundary between the two areas. For members of a marginalized group whose voices and views are not acknowledged in the larger public sphere, what is personal easily intertwines with what is political. Smith provides further delineation of this idea when she presents Aída Hurtado's thoughts about the connection between women of color and the public and private spheres; that their political consciousness arises from "an awareness that the public is *personally* political."[50] Moreover, Hurtado maintains that the only private sphere that exists for people of color is the one they are able to "create and protect in an otherwise hostile environment."[51] If this is the case, then the public and the private are fused together in the eyes of the member of the marginalized public sphere. And failing to (re)present the standpoint that is part of this fused private/public sphere in the larger public sphere means failing to (re)present the identity of that person. Such a failure indicates a devaluation of the identity of the members of that public/private sphere. *Volunteer Slavery* shows how Nelson's identity as a "race woman"—the very thing she assumed she was hired to be—is devalued. First, after the African American community begins its protest of the magazine after the "Murder, Drugs, and the Rap Star" article, she is effectively cut off from African American readers because she works for the *Post*. As she tells Jay Lovinger, "Most black people won't talk to me until the demonstrations are over, and those that will make me promise not to publish the piece until the problem is resolved."[52] She views herself as a "corporate sellout, a traitor, an Uncle Tom."[53]

Next, she has to deal with editors who devalue the very thing that comprises a reporter's identity in the newsroom: her work. After a few months at the paper, she realizes that she is "just about invisible" unless she acts out, "in which case, I am treated like an intimidating, overbearing, frightening-type black."[54] Furthermore, her feelings of invisibility are exacerbated by the fact that no one seems to care about the fact that she is "visible but invisible" because of her race and gender:

> It seems enough that I am here, black and female. No one but me feels it necessary that I actually do anything. As long as I can say that I am "working on" something, everyone is cool.
> Everyone but me, that is.[55]

Hurtado also argues that the "relative positionality" of specific groups of women to the "middle-class white man" needs to be examined in order to determine the ways in which standpoints are presented.[56] The "middle-class white man" is the "prototype for the universal subject" who dominates the center of the public sphere and whose standpoint determines the places of power, the margins of meaning, and the geographies of knowledge. As a result, the proximity of members of marginalized groups to the "universal subject" has to be considered; different proximities to the dominant private sphere result in different cultural ways of defining gender and different cultural practices of gender, leading to conflicts between women whose relationships to power differ. This suggests that white women, being closer in sociopolitical proximity to white men than black women are, may have conflicted relationships with black women they supervise. In *Volunteer Slavery*, this is reflected when Nelson describes her relationship with her editor—the "white feminist"—to Jay Lovinger: "She rewrites my quotes. She gives me editorial instructions, not suggestions. . . . [S]he's rude and has no respect for me."[57] The frustrations she feels in her dealings with her editor do not, perhaps, differ from editor-reporter clashes in any newsroom, but they are exacerbated by the fact the editor who is supposed to be Neslon's advocate, based on shared assumptions of gender, adds to the feelings of invisibility and marginalization Nelson experiences in her first few months on the job. Added to this marginalization is the fact that Lovinger refuses to tackle the situation directly, instead suggesting that Nelson work with a black editor. This is a suggestion with which she disagrees. The problem, as she sees it, is about ability:

> [Lovinger] continues talking about my need for a black editor. I bite my lip and try not to let my mouth fall open. . . . Because if my lips part I'm likely to say, "Look, I know I'm black and I know I'm female, that's no revelation. What the hell does that have to do with editing my work? I mean, do we rewrite quotes here or what? That's what I wanna know; that's not a racial or sexual issue, is it? There's nothing wrong with me; I need a good editor."[58]

In the end, what Nelson announces in *Volunteer Slavery* is her presence. Her autobiography becomes a site from which she makes a statement about her existence in the setting of the corporate newsroom. She uses her text to cut through the visible-invisibility she experiences as a reporter inside the newsroom—and as a *black* reporter working for a white newspaper outside the newsroom, where she is considered "part of the problem" by those in the African American community who are protesting the paper.[59] Inside the newsroom, she is "just the spook who sits by the door," a bird in a gilded cage who eventually grows tired of her isolation.[60] She writes,

> I pretty much do what I want, come and go as I please. It's as if now that I've integrated the staff, I needn't do much else. This is fun for a few

weeks, but then it gets tired. After all, I came here to write and be successful. I'm willing to be a token, but not an unused one. I figure everyone,
including white men, gets hired because of who they are. It's just that
because white men run things, they're only able to pretend that when they
hire one another, they do so based on merit; when they hire a black person
or woman, they're doing us a favor.

I feel comfortable getting in the door because I am a spook, but I don't
intend to sit by it.[61]

She is willing to accede to the demands that tokenism requires.
After all, tokenism would allow a space for her writing to be presented.
However, Neslon feels that "token" status should not lead to marginalization. And her intention to become visible is made manifest not
just in the statement of her intention to speak to her supervisor about
her problems with her editor. It is also manifested in the writing—and
subsequent publication—of an autobiographical text. The text is a space
in which she "performs" visibility by writing about her experiences in
confronting it. Among the ways in which Nelson performs is her choice
of title, a reference to the song by Rahsaan Roland Kirk.[62] She uses it
to refer to the way she perceives her status at the *Post*. In the book, she
presents a scene in which she sings along to the song and reflects on her
state after the protest of the *Post* magazine begins:

> I'm a volunteer slave, a buppie. My price? A house, a Volvo, and the il-
> lusion of disposable income. When it's lights out, I convince myself that
> the quantity of the work I do justifies where and for whom I do it. It's in
> the darkness, black like me, that it's hard. I hurry home to drown my self-
> disgust in Russian vodka and pray for Harriet Tubman's arrival.[63]

She performs self-analysis and does not like what she sees. Whether
the audience accepts or understands her performance is irrelevant; it is
grounded in her memory of her experience. Furthermore, performance
is also grounded in history, and, as a result, so is identity. Smith argues
that by "historicizing" identity, "the autobiographical manifesto implicitly, if not explicitly, insists on the temporalities and spatial identities
of identity, and, in doing so, brings the everyday practices of identity
directly into the floodlights of conscious display."[64] In *Volunteer Slavery*
this is evident in Nelson's reference to Harriet Tubman, who is mentioned because Nelson wishes to be freed from her "volunteer slavery."
The reporters at the newspaper's outlying bureaus are described as being

exiled to a "reportorial Elba," where they hope, mostly in vain, to regain the lost luster of their once-promising careers. Most significantly, in the same instance, Nelson uses a reference to South Africa's Voortrekkers to define the newspaper's position and her situation during the magazine backlash and protest. She writes,

> In South Africa a hundred years ago, the Voortrekkers called it the "white lager." That's when they pulled their wagons in a circle, hunkered down, and prepared to defend themselves against the encroaching African hordes who had the audacity to fight for their land.
>   At the *Washington Post* magazine, the caucasians [*sic*] didn't call it anything, but as far as I was concerned, it was the white lager circa 1986. There I was, an African-American woman, caught in the middle of a bunch of circling white wagons.[65]

More than a historical reference, Nelson's description reinforces the sense of isolation that she feels like a "volunteer slave" because of the conflicted relationship between her race and her chosen profession. The Voortrekkers are symbolic of the way she feels trapped within the circle of wagons that is the newspaper management's mistake in judgment and isolated from—but also shielded from—what she sees is the justifiable anger of protesters.

Volunteer Slavery shows how the autobiographical manifesto announces "the politicization of the private and the personalization of the public."[66] Personal issues become political ones, and the autobiography becomes the site where the member of a marginalized public sphere can expose the problems within the larger, un-marginalized public sphere. It is a place where standpoints can be presented, assessed, and discussed. The result is the upsetting of the public/private dichotomy of selfhood favored by the ancien régime.[67] The autobiographical manifesto challenges the hegemonic notions of common sense and identity constructed in a public sphere that stifles marginalized standpoints.

Notes

1. Ted Pease and Guido H. Stempel, "Striving to the Top: Views of Minority Newspaper Executives," Newspaper Research Journal 11 (1990), 64–79.
2. Carol M. Liebler, "How Race and Gender Affect Journalists' Autonomy," Newspaper Research Journal 15, no. 3 (1994).

3. Richard Gross, Patricia A. Curtin, and Glen T. Cameron, "Diversity Advances Both Journalism, Business," Newspaper Research Journal 22, no. 2 (2001).

4. Paul John Eakin, *How Our Lives Become Stories: Making Selves*, Cornell Paperbacks (Ithaca, NY: Cornell University Press, 1999), 43.

5. Janet Lyon, *Manifestoes: Provocations of the Modern* (Ithaca, NY: Cornell University Press, 1999), 8.

6. John Hartley, *Communication, Cultural and Media Studies: The Key Concepts*, 3rd ed., Routledge Key Guides (London: Routledge, 2002), 149. Hartley states that after an interrupted English experiment in democratic government from 1645 to 1700, political modernity in the West was successfully implemented—in an ongoing form—with the American and French revolutions in 1776 and 1789.

7. Lyon, *Manifestoes*, 8.

8. Lyon, *Manifestoes*, 9

9. Lyon, *Manifestoes*, 9.

10. Lyon, *Manifestoes*, 10.

11. Sidonie Smith, "Autobiographical Manifestos," in *Women, Autobiography, Theory: A Reader*, ed. Sidonie Smith and Julia Watson, Wisconsin Studies in American Autobiography (Madison: University of Wisconsin Press, 1998), 435.

12. Smith, "Autobiographical Manifestos," 433.

13. Smith, "Autobiographical Manifestos," 435.

14. Smith, "Autobiographical Manifestos," 435.

15. Smith, "Autobiographical Manifestos," 435.

16. Joanne M. Braxton, *Black Women Writing Autobiography: A Tradition within a Tradition* (Philadelphia: Temple University Press, 1989), 9.

17. Jill Nelson, *Volunteer Slavery: My Authentic Negro Experience* (New York: Penguin, 1993), 4.

18. Nelson, *Volunteer Slavery*, 5.

19. Nelson, *Volunteer Slavery*, 5.

20. Nelson, *Volunteer Slavery* 6–7.

21. Nelson, *Volunteer Slavery*, 42. The Post also added her to the payroll before she actually began working there. Later she realized that this was a ploy to improve its diversity numbers for a report the paper submitted to the EEOC.

22. Nelson, *Volunteer Slavery*, 53.

23. Nelson, *Volunteer Slavery*, 53. Bigger Thomas was the protagonist of Wright's novel *Native Son*. In the novel, Bigger accidentally kills a young white woman and, in an effort to conceal his crime, tries to dispose of the body by incinerating it.

24. Nelson, *Volunteer Slavery*, 53.

25. Nelson, *Volunteer Slavery*, 53.

26. Nelson, *Volunteer Slavery*, 53.

27. Nelson, *Volunteer Slavery*, 54.

28. Nelson, *Volunteer Slavery*, 59–60.

29. Pamela Newkirk, *Within the Veil: Black Journalists, White Media* (New York: New York University Press, 2000), 7.

30. Nelson, *Volunteer Slavery*, 54.

31. Smith, "Autobiographical Manifestos," 435.

32. Smith, "Autobiographical Manifestos," 436.

33. Smith, "Autobiographical Manifestos," 436.

34. John Sturrock, *The Language of Autobiography: Studies in the First Person Singular* (New York: Cambridge University Press, 1993), 12.

35. Nancy C. M. Hartsock, "Foucault on Power: A Theory for Women," in *Feminism/Postmodernism*, ed. Linda J. Nicholson, Thinking Gender (New York: Routledge, 1990), 160–61.

36. Nelson, *Volunteer Slavery*, 57.

37. Nelson, *Volunteer Slavery*, 61.

38. Nelson, *Volunteer Slavery*, 62–63.

39. Nelson, *Volunteer Slavery*, 62.

40. Nelson, *Volunteer Slavery*, 62.

41. Nelson, *Volunteer Slavery*, 35.

42. Nelson, *Volunteer Slavery*, 35.

43. Nelson, *Volunteer Slavery*, 36.

44. Nelson, *Volunteer Slavery*, 36.

45. Jannette L. Dates and Edward C. Pease, "Warping the World: Media's Mangled Images of Race," *Media Studies Journal* 8, no. 3 (1994): 89–90.

46. Smith, "Autobiographical Manifestos," 436.

47. Kenneth Mostern, *Autobiography and Black Identity Politics: Racialization in Twentieth-Century America*, Cultural Margins, no. 7 (New York: Cambridge University Press, 1999), 11.

48. Smith, "Autobiographical Manifestos," 437.

49. Smith, "Autobiographical Manifestos," 436.

50. Smith, "Autobiographical Manifestos," 436.

51. Smith, "Autobiographical Manifestos," 436.

52. Nelson, *Volunteer Slavery*, 79.

53. Nelson, *Volunteer Slavery*, 78.

54. Nelson, *Volunteer Slavery*, 78.

55. Nelson, *Volunteer Slavery*, 78.

56. Smith, "Autobiographical Manifestos," 436. Because previous theories about feminism have predominantly emphasized the lives and experiences of middle-class white women, Hurtado proposes the theory of relational privilege to explain the differing conceptions of feminism by women in different racial

and/or ethnic groups. She posits that the different responses to feminism by women of color do not stem from personality or cultural differences between white women and women of color, but instead from their differing connections to white men—with white women having closer connections and therefore more relational privilege. To her, subordination and are privilege relational in nature and need to be examined in contexts of culture and socioeconomics. Aída Hurtado, *The Color of Privilege: Three Blasphemies on Race and Feminism,* Critical Perspectives on Women and Gender (Ann Arbor: University of Michigan Press, 1996).

57. Nelson, *Volunteer Slavery,* 80.

58. Nelson, *Volunteer Slavery,* 80

59. Nelson, *Volunteer Slavery,* 74. Nelson is stopped on her way to work by one of the protesters. After discovering that she works for the Post, he accuses her of spying for the paper and demands to know her stance on the magazine situation. Before she can fully explain her position, he references author-activist Eldridge Cleaver's statement that "[i]f you're not part of the solution, you're part of the problem" (73).

60. Nelson, *Volunteer Slavery,* 79. Nelson's statement is a reference to the novel *The Spook Who Sat by the Door* by Sam Greenlee, a satire about an African American CIA operative who, after becoming dissatisfied with his token status, leaves the agency and begins recruiting young inner-city men and training them in the counterintelligence techniques he learned.

61. Nelson, *Volunteer Slavery,* 79.

62. The lines from the lyrics she quotes in the text are "Oh, volunteer slavery/It's something we all know/Oh, volunteer slavery, oh, volunteer slavery." Nelson, *Volunteer Slavery,* 67.

63. Nelson, *Volunteer Slavery,* 67.

64. Smith, "Autobiographical Manifestos," 437.

65. Nelson, *Volunteer Slavery,* 67.

66. Smith, "Autobiographical Manifestos," 436–37.

67. Smith, "Autobiographical Manifestos," 437.

3

Volunteer Slavery and the Speech Aspects of the Autobiographical Manifesto

V OLUNTEER SLAVERY ILLUMINATES THE SYNERGISTIC RELATIONSHIP between the categories of race, gender, class, and profession that allows the text to function as an autobiographical manifesto. That is, these categories work together in the text in ways that allow it to transcend memoir and become instead autobiographical manifesto. In this chapter I continue the analysis of Jill Nelson's memoir by examining the two final constituent aspects of autobiographical manifestos as they present themselves in the work: (1) to speak as one of a group/for a group and (2) to speak to the future. I am exploring these two aspects separately because I posit that they are the most important part of the auto-biographical manifesto. They are important because they determine the voice of the author and direction for the future action a manifesto necessarily demands. The manifesto voice presents an understood or stated "we" versus "they" in which the terms of conflict are constructed in a "deliberate dichotomy."[1] It suggests directions for future action by positioning itself between "what has been done and what will be done, between the accomplished and the potential."[2] The manifesto is a Janus-faced document that looks both back to the past and forward to the future. The autobiographical manifesto presents a life story that situates itself in a moment of time and looks back at a life lived while suggesting for its audience future paths for accomplishment and action.

Memoir and Group Member Speech

The penultimate characteristic of autobiographical manifestos is to speak as one of a group, to speak for a group. For the manifesto, it is group membership rather than radical individuality that serves as the rhetorical ground of appeal.[3] During public performance of the life narrative, the speaker is positioned specifically within the membership of a group or community; the specifically positioned individual, "anchored in collectivity," becomes a counter-public sphere.[4] By aligning him- or herself within the membership of a group or community, the author's text becomes a site of reaction against the dominant public sphere.

Sidonie Smith maintains that there exist myriad counter-public spheres, all connected to a variety of experiences of oppression and exclusion from the main public sphere and its concept of the universal "I." Furthermore, as Joan Scott asserts, the subjects in autobiographies are shaped through discourse, through the social processes involved in making and remaking sense, but conflicts exist among and contradictions exist within discursive systems, allowing for multiple meanings, multiple ways of seeing.[5] If this is true, then there are, of course, a number of standpoints, each ready to offer a valid critique of the dominant public sphere, whose hegemonic influence over the shape of discourse renders the members of the counter-public sphere as outsiders.

Accordingly, in order to "speak as one of a group," the subject of the autobiographical manifesto "speaks as a member of a nonhegemonic group or counter-public sphere," a group that has its own languages and discursive modes of interaction.[6] And because subjects have agency, and discourse is both a shared event and a shared action, "experience is collective as well as individual."[7] To speak for a group, on the other hand, means to speak as one who sympathizes with the issues of concern to a marginalized public, without necessarily having membership in that public. This can work because there is an understanding that in order to have sympathy with the issues of a marginalized group in their counter-public sphere, one must have at least studied the discourses created by members of the group. To fail to do so yet still attempt to speak for a group results in demagoguery.

In the tradition of African American autobiography, the tendency of its subjects is to speak *as members of* a group instead of *for* a group. African American subjects present their lives to the public as individuals who represent a whole group. The tradition from which African American autobiography arises is one that maintains that autobiography is one of the ways in which sociopolitical and cultural issues can be debated and changed. According to William Andrews,

> Nineteenth-century abolitionists sponsored the publication of the narratives of escaped slaves out of a conviction that first-person accounts of those victimized by and yet triumphant over slavery would mobilize white readers more profoundly than any other kind of antislavery discourse. . . . It was the narratives of self-styled black revolutionaries in the 1960s and early 1970s that compelled the American academy to reconsider widespread assumptions about literature's transcendent relationship to social struggle.[8]

Thus, when African American autobiographers present their life writings, they are tapping into a long-standing tradition of using life stories to present perspectives on the world that are unknown or ignored in the larger society. They are explorations and presentations of standpoints. The authors appropriate the form of the autobiography to bring to light issues of concern as a means of public announcement while speaking as one of a group whose standpoints have not been examined.

Jill Nelson and the other African American journalists whose life writings are being examined in the succeeding chapters are members of an important set of nonhegemonic groups. First, they are African Americans, which means that as autobiographers, they are immediately connected to the tradition of autobiography that is itself part of the African American literary tradition. Second, they are journalists, a term that has a multitude of usable definitions. However, journalism historian Rodger Streitmatter provides a most appropriate one when he defines a journalist as someone whose nonfiction work is disseminated to a wide audience in a regularly appearing publication.[9] Journalists are members of a group who consider themselves professionals, an attitude that paralleled the emergence in the late 1800s of what David Mindich calls the "'objective' ethic."[10] Because journalists believe they have professional status, they also believe it accords them particular privileges that accompany that status. This includes, as Howard Good states, the privilege of writing autobiographies.[11] Consequently, for Nelson and other journalist-autobiographers who are black, the appropriation of an autobiographical space is legitimized based not only on cultural-historical tradition, but also on professional entitlement. So they become associated with a host of other members of the profession—male and female, from a variety of ethnic and racial backgrounds—who have used the autobiographical form to take their life stories and—through the re-creation, stretching, shaping, and transforming of experience—create coherence. The result of this coherence-making process is a creative work.

It is immediately apparent from the title of her text that race is an important component to the story in Nelson's memoir. The title, *Volunteer Slavery*, alludes to a song, and its use in the title situates her experience in a particular African American experience that is part of the cultural memory of black people. But Nelson's focus is on the dehumanizing aspect of slavery as a metaphor for her experience as an African American woman in the corporate newsroom. It would be an easy leap to focus on the "volunteer" aspect of the title in critiquing the book, dismissing Nelson as a whiner who should have known what she was getting into and who was probably destined to leave the *Post* as she did from the day she first walked into Ben Bradlee's office. But that would undercut understanding of the idea that just because one volunteers for something does not give another person carte blanche to take advantage of him or her.

Nelson extends the slavery connection to her experience by referencing history. But her references go beyond mere allusions. For example, when she becomes concerned that complaining to management about her editor may lead to trouble and says, "The white lager at the magazine realizes that not only am I not Mammy, I may be part of Nat Turner's gang," she reveals not only how she sees herself, but also how others see her.[12] It foreshadows her treatment by the editors later in her tenure at the paper. It is an effective standpoint critique of the ways in which power in the newsroom affects those who are powerless but not voiceless.

Beyond her racial identification, Nelson's group identity is complicated by her gender. *Volunteer Slavery* is the story of a woman's search for "authentic Negro experiences" and the role journalism plays in that search. It is a singular journey, but it is complicated by the fact that, as she notes many times in the book, Nelson identifies herself as a "race woman." In doing so, she harkens back to a tradition that is a hallmark of African American women journalists—Ida B. Wells, Charlotta Bass, and Charlayne Hunter-Gault are prominent examples—and African American women in general, who, as Streitmatter states, "historically have identified themselves first as members of an oppressed race, feeling the pain of racial prejudice more acutely than the pain of sexual prejudice."[13] Thus, it seems that Nelson has chosen to speak as a member of a group: African American women who are engaged in pursuit of racial reform and the attendant acknowledgment of cultural worth. This gives her a definition of herself outside her work context. But her quest is an intensely dichotomized one, as she struggles to define herself within the context of her professional newsroom experiences. Unlike Frederick Douglass and Harriet Jacobs, whose autobiographical works expose the oppression extant in a system into which they were subjugated against their will, Nelson's "slavery" is voluntary because she has chosen to submit herself to the source of the marginalization about which she writes. In order to expose, she must participate; in order to speak as a member of a group, she must position herself between groups as a voice.

The subject of gender is connected to the subject of race because Nelson sees herself as a self-styled "race woman" in the tradition of many other African American female journalists. Additionally, Nelson the autobiographer is part of a tradition of African American women writers who use autobiography and their standpoints as victims of "black and white, male and female dominance" to critique power relations in American society and to define themselves. As Nellie McKay writes,

> Twentieth-century daughters and granddaughters of earlier "scribbling" black women continue to write themselves through issues of individual and collective survival in a world that still denigrates blackness and privileges maleness over femaleness.[14]

Again, gender, like race, has a historical component that informs African American autobiography. For Nelson, class is important to her story because it is something she struggles with throughout her experience at the *Post*. Class and its influence on cultural identity comprise the underlying theme of *Volunteer Slavery*. Raised on Manhattan's Upper West Side and the daughter of a dentist and a librarian, Nelson believes her middle-class upbringing keeps her from "authentic" black experiences. Even her interview at the *Post* lacked authenticity: To her, Bradlee seemed interested in her only once she mentioned spending summers in Martha's Vineyard. She concludes that such an association separated her from the "otherness" of being black, making her acceptable to whites. But throughout her time at the post, it was her blackness that was threatened by the management. Her viewpoint was devalued. Her standpoint was rendered irrelevant.

An even further complication in Nelson's group identity exists along the fault line of class. Nelson is not only a "race woman," she is a race woman who is a member of the black middle class. Thus, it seems that her allegiances would be split among the categories of race, gender, and class. But this complication in her group identity is mitigated as well by the race woman identity. Moreover, membership in the black middle class historically has not made individuals immune from the effects of racial discrimination. In fact, as Ellis Cose contends,

> Despite its very evident prosperity, much of America's black middle class is in excruciating pain. And that distress—although most of the country does not see it—illuminates a serious American problem: the problem of the broken covenant, of the pact ensuring that if you work hard, get a good education, and play by the rules, you will be allowed to advance and achieve to the limits of your ability.[15]

So for members of the black middle class, issues involving racial justice are still salient concerns that need to be addressed in the public sphere, even though there are those who claim that American society has progressed toward a "post-racial" America as a result of the 2008 presidential election. Autobiography provides one way of accomplishing this task. Autobiographers who are members of the black middle class have the advantage of being able to appropriate a sanctioned socioeconomic space that affords some measure of sovereignty in the public sphere. Seen as having "made it" in the eyes of those who inhabit the larger public sphere, members of the black middle class can more effectively use the autobiographical space to bring to light issues of importance and illuminate ways in which the "covenant" that is part of the "American Dream" is not being upheld.

On the whole, to speak as one of a group and/or for a group means to appropriate a space for dialogue between public spheres. It means to assume a shared identity in order to present issues of concern or to present a particular standpoint. If, as Smith contends, the individual stories presented in an autobiographical manifesto become the occasion for social critique via standpoint epistemology, then it is the speaker's identity as one of the group or as the avatar of a group that signifies the voice of these critiques.

The Promise of the Future

In order to contextualize the final characteristic of autobiographical manifestos—"to speak to the future"—Smith presents the following ideas about the place of autobiography in relation to the whole of literary practice:

> The generic contracts of western literary practices promise something, but what exactly they promise is subject to various theoretical interpretations. Traditionally, western autobiography involves a contractual obligation in which the autobiographer engages in a narrative itinerary of self-disclosure, retrospective summation, self-justification.[16]

It is a tradition, then, that any text that purports to be literary in nature must promise something to its readers. And though the underlying idea of this study is the focus on autobiographies as nonliterary, quasi-political statements, I would be remiss to completely dissociate the texts from their literary connections. As has been previously discussed, the autobiographies in this study reflect an African American tradition of writing in which, according to Houston A. Baker, the "generative conditions of diasporic African life that privilege spiritual negotiation and the work of consciousness also make autobiography the premier genre of Afro-American discourse."[17] They emerge out of a tradition that exists as a reaction to—and in reflection of—Western literary tradition. As such, African American autobiographers engage in the same acts of self-disclosure, retrospective summation, and self-justification as other autobiographers.

However, authors' purposes have deeper meaning because of the nature of the subject's identity. As described previously, the individual identities of African American autobiographers are conjoined with the racial group identity. So their acts of disclosure, summation, and justification always have the goal of revealing for the larger public the ways in which racial injustices are enacted in society.

In general, autobiographies focus on relating past events and recasting those events in whatever light the subject sees fit to use to illuminate them; they are also about the future. Furthermore, the subject in the autobiographical manifesto "does not write under the sign of desire or the sign of anxiety," but instead he or she writes "under the sign of hope" and the possibility of change, with a focus on what Smith calls the "generative and prospective thrust of autobiography."[18]

Furthermore, inherent in the manifesto is a particular forward-thinking focus that is especially important to members of marginalized groups. According to Janet Lyon:

> In shifting the culture of a marginalized group, the manifesto yields an alternative historical narrative, one that foregrounds the group's grievances and thereby struggles squarely within but also in opposition to a culture's foundational narratives. "Our history is the unthought chapter in your history," declares the manifesto to its opponents, "and now your history will be justly superseded by our unfolding future."[19]

Accordingly, autobiographical manifestos reveal the past in order to suggest a course for the future—as African American autobiographies traditionally have done. Autobiographical manifestos do so by repositioning the subject in a liberated future, away from the constraints and oppressions practiced on a day-to-day basis by the ancien régime.[20]

Volunteer Slavery functions as an autobiographical manifesto whose purpose is to explore the conflicted nature of the "authentic" black self as shaped in the personal, family, and professional realms of being. However, there is a particular event in her past that allows Jill Nelson to speak to/about the future. This event, presented in chapter 21, involves a statement made by her ex-husband—"the plump, economically solvent wannabee"—and sets up the underlying theme of the final chapters of the autobiography, which cover the end of Nelson's time at the *Post*:

> There was only one incisive thing the Ex-Husband ever said that I can remember. This utterance occurred one August day on Martha's Vineyard after we'd parked and swam in Ice House Pond, which is located on private property, and returned to the car to find that it wouldn't start because someone had taken the distributor cap. "Someone" turned out to be the white man who owned land and the pond, who eventually emerged from the surrounding woods like some character from *Deliverance*, gave us a stern lecture on the rights of property owners and returned the distributor cap. That's when my husband said, "You know, there's nothing worse than being wrong around white folks."[21]

Nelson uses this incident to reflect upon one of the pitfalls of being black and working in corporate America:

We spend a great deal of time trying to be perfect, to never make mistakes around white folks, because when we do we suspect those mistakes go into an amorphous White Folks Sin Bank Against The Negro. We fear that, once discovered, our little *faux pas* is stored in the same bank with the really scary sins—also imaginary—of Angela Davis, Alton Maddox, and Malcolm and Martin, before they were killed and turned into harmless T-shirt icons.[22]

Through her statement, she describes the present—*her* present— comments on the past, and speaks to the future, even as she issues a warning to those who may enter the corporate workplace. For African Americans in the corporate workplace, then, the wages of "sin" is, in- deed, death—death of the self, as one's individuality is deposited into the "White Folks Sin Bank" with as much thought as one tosses a coin into a jar of other coins.

The "sin" Nelson commits takes place during an assignment in which she plans to interview one of her former teachers for a story. She signs the initials of Steve Petranek, the magazine's managing editor, on a voucher for the rental car she is driving to do the interview for the story. (He is in a meeting with other editors at the time she goes to fill out the form.) Realizing that she has possibly committed a breach in procedure, she later takes another voucher to Petranek, who, after signing it, shows her the form she filled out before. He then proceeds to accuse her "of forgery and trying to defraud the Washington Post Company."[23] Her explanations that the trip was preapproved and that she did not try to imitate Petranek's signature or deceive anyone are ignored. After a meeting with *Post* editor Ben Bradlee, she is given one week's suspen- sion without pay and the story is killed. Nelson reflects on the incident and its connection to the incident with her ex-husband and the car.

Ultimately, she realizes that even though the paper has overreacted to her misstep, and she feels that management is punishing her "for crimes other than the one at hand," the "ultimate crime" is what she calls the "sin of being less than perfect, of making a mistake . . . of being wrong around white folks."[24] She provides a deposit for the "Sin Bank" and becomes an example for whites of what happens when a member of a marginalized public sphere is allowed to have power within an institution controlled by members of the dominant public sphere. For members of the dominant public sphere, Nelson's actions, however un- intentional and essentially benign, become evidence of standpoint run

amok, wherein the sociocultural perspectives of the marginalized public
are looked at as being so different that even their interpretation of rules
of ethics are called into question. This allows members of the dominant
class to validate their marginalization of the "other."

The autobiographical manifesto is a text that not only looks back,
but also "gestures forward in 'the affirmative positivity of its politics'
to new spaces for subjectivity."[25] In addition to carving out paths that
suggest new, more positive, more inclusive politics, autobiographical
manifestos are also texts that set out new ways of writing about self.
Volunteer Slavery fails at this task. But that does not mean the work fails
as autobiographical manifesto. The main qualities of autobiographical
manifesto exist in such abundance as to offset its lack of pathfinding
potential. Nelson's discussion of her experiences speaks to the future by
describing "what is"—the old adage that an employee who is a member
of a marginalized group has to work twice as hard to be considered half
as good as someone from a nonmarginalized group. So what is true for
Nelson in her experience is what has been true in the past for others and
what will be true for others in the future. By the end of her autobiography, what Nelson learns and presents for the future is the idea that her
"authentic" self is a relational self formed by her roles as mother, daugh-
ter/sister, and journalist. But that self is constrained by the demands of
the mainstream corporate newsroom that, despite appearing to value
different viewpoints, is often inimical to different viewpoints—or to
anyone who might be too insistent on presenting a standpoint that con-
tradicts the shared values of the newsroom. These values are defined and
reinforced by members of the dominant public sphere who have shared
values and a shared—if not complete—history.

Notes

1. Mary Ann Caws, *Manifesto: A Century of Isms* (Lincoln: University of
Nebraska Press, 2001), xx.

2. Caws, *Manifesto*, xxi.

3. Sidonie Smith, "Autobiographical Manifestos," in *Women, Autobiography, Theory: A Reader*, ed. Sidonie Smith and Julia Watson, Wisconsin Studies
in American Autobiography (Madison: University of Wisconsin Press, 1998),
437.

4. Smith, "Autobiographical Manifestos," 437.

5. Joan Scott, "Experience," in *Feminists Theorize the Political*, ed. Judith Butler and Joan Scott (New York: Routledge, 1992), 33.

6. Smith, "Autobiographical Manifestos."

7. Scott, "Experience," 34.

8. William L. Andrews, *African American Autobiography: A Collection of Critical Essays*, New Century Views (Englewood Cliffs, NJ: Prentice Hall, 1993), 2.

9. Rodger Streitmatter, *Raising Her Voice: African-American Women Journalists Who Changed History* (Lexington: University Press of Kentucky, 1994), 8.

10. David T. Z. Mindich, *Just the Facts: How "Objectivity" Came to Define American Journalism* (New York: New York University Press, 1998), 115.

11. Howard Good, *The Journalist as Autobiographer* (Metuchen, NJ: Scarecrow Press, 1993), 2.

12. Jill Nelson, *Volunteer Slavery: My Authentic Negro Experience* (New York: Penguin, 1993), 93.

13. Streitmatter, *Raising Her Voice*, 10.

14. Nellie McKay, "The Narrative Self: Race, Politics, and Culture in Black American Women's Autobiography," in *Feminisms in the Academy*, ed. Domna C. Stanton and Abigail J. Stewart (Ann Arbor: University of Michigan Press, 1995), 100.

15. Ellis Cose, *The Rage of a Privileged Class* (New York: HarperCollins, 1993), 1.

16. Smith, "Autobiographical Manifestos," 438.

17. Houston A. Baker, "Theoretical Returns," in *African American Literary Theory: A Reader*, ed. Winston Napier (New York: New York University Press, 2000), 422.

18. Smith, "Autobiographical Manifestos," 438.

19. Janet Lyon, *Manifestoes: Provocations of the Modern* (Ithaca, NY: Cornell University Press, 1999), 15.

20. Smith, "Autobiographical Manifestos," 438.

21. Nelson, *Volunteer Slavery*, 149.

22. Nelson, *Volunteer Slavery*, 150.

23. Nelson, *Volunteer Slavery*, 152.

24. Nelson, *Volunteer Slavery*, 155. Among the other "crimes" to which Nelson refers is the fact that before the voucher incident, the *Post* unit of the Baltimore-Washington Newspaper Guild, of which she was the chair, filed a discrimination complaint against the paper.

25. Smith, "Autobiographical Manifestos," 438.

4

Surveillance and Performance in Nathan McCall's *Makes Me Wanna Holler*

W HEN JILL NELSON REVIEWED Nathan McCall's 1994 memoir *Makes Me Wanna Holler: A Young Black Man in America* for the *Nation*, she described McCall's book as "[c]hockfull of details sometimes bordering on the trivial," but noted that as McCall recalls the events of importance in his life, he fails to give readers the "introspection and sense of process to understand that life."[1] McCall's work is his story about his struggles and successes in a white world as a black man, including his steady ascent to the *Washington Post* and the struggles he endured during his work at the paper. In addition to presenting his life, he uses his memoir to illuminate the ongoing newsroom wars he observed between white men and white women—a process, he feels, by which black journalists are excluded from real power.[2]

McCall, Sovereignty, and Surveillance

Like the title of Nelson's book, the title of McCall's book is an allusion to a song, specifically the Marvin Gaye song "Inner City Blues (Makes Me Wanna Holler)," but McCall does not have to appropriate sovereignty in the same way Nelson does. Even though he is African American, he is a male, and, at least within the African American public sphere, still has access to the kinds of social power that are inherent in a social structure that endorses patriarchal control. However, instead of existing on the same plane as the white male patriarchal power, black male patriarchal power parallels the patriarchal control that is part of white culture, the type of ancien régime against which autobiographical manifestos react. *Makes Me Wanna Holler,* indeed, is about being black and being male in a society that devalues black maleness, especially when the black male has served time in prison, as McCall has. Because of his double-devaluation, McCall has to reappropriate a level of sovereignty that is typically assumed within a patriarchal context. Like *Volunteer Slavery, Makes Me Wanna Holler* is about a personal quest. The author tries to define what it means to be a black man by trying to define himself. The identity he tries to define is a relational self that, by part 3 of the book (which is the main focus of this discussion), is shaped by many interactions with people—as a son, a father, a friend, a student, a lover, an inmate, a reporter.

Unlike Nelson, however, McCall does not try to contest the sovereignty of the double-consciousness paradigm. Nelson's pursuit of a single, "authentic" self is not so much about looking at herself through what Du Bois says is "the revelation of the other world"—the way others, namely whites, see her—she is trying to find it by looking at herself through herself—the other world merely serves as an impediment to her quest for an authentic Negro self. For McCall, the idea of revelation of self through other worlds or through the actions of others is an ever-present theme of the experiences he discusses, particularly in part 3. He is always aware of the fact that he exists in two worlds; he is both insider and outsider. He learns about the world by letting it reveal itself to him. In chapter 19, McCall describes how he gained insight by observing the actions at Southampton Correctional Center, where he served three years:

> In those first few months in C-1 [the building where he is incarcerated at Southampton], I spent a lot of time taking the pulse of prison life, learning to identify the wolves, the hustlers, the thumpers, the loudmouth bluffs, the thieves, and the few progressive inmates in my building. From my second-floor perch, I saw all kinds of transactions among guys handing off contraband and paying off debts with cigarettes and cookies as they passed each other on the first floor.
>
> By watching others' mistakes, I also learned some of the dos and don'ts of prison life: like don't be seen getting too chummy with administrators—it makes the hustlers paranoid.[3]

McCall's view of the prison is a Foucauldian, panoptic one in that he observes the actions of all the prisoners at once, garnering from them information he needs to survive. It is a view in which the other inmates' actions become "so many small theatres, in which each actor is alone, perfectly individualized and constantly visible."[4] The other prisoners become objects of information instead of subjects in communication. As objects of information, their actions empower McCall by helping him learn to navigate the prison environment and by helping him reappropriate and contest sovereignty as the author of an autobiographical text. By writing about his actions, he appropriates sovereignty because he gains the identity of survivor and his actions serve as a testament to that fact. As a survivor who later goes on and works in the mainstream press, he contests the sovereignty of those who may consider his identity as a citizen a tainted, unredeemable one.

An important issue McCall brings to light deals with identity: How much should our personal history impact our future? How much of our personal history should we hide in order to survive in society? McCall has to deal with these questions when he decides to become a journalist. Three years after his release from prison, he graduates from college with a degree in journalism and decides to pursue a career as a journalist. During an interview session with the *Louisville Courier-Journal*, he tells the personnel director about his prison record, although he did not write it down on the application. After a brief discussion with her supervisors, the personnel manager dismisses McCall, who realizes that he will not land the job:

> I don't remember what, if any, reason they gave for not hiring me, but I'm sure that it was because I came clean. I couldn't handle that. I'd served my time. I'd been punished for the crime and suffered, I thought, more than enough. I wondered, Why do I have to keep paying for it, and what benefit is there in me telling interviewers the truth?[5]

After the incident, McCall decides that he would not disclose the details about his prison stint to future employers. "I'd get my foot in the door first and prove myself," he writes. "Then maybe, maybe, I'd tell them about my past."[6] However, he ends up having to disclose his prison record to the editors at the *Virginian Pilot-Leger Star*, the paper that eventually hires him in 1981 after his other job prospects fail to materialize. But he later keeps his vow when he moves to the *Atlanta*

Journal-Constitution. There, he builds a record of accomplishment as a reporter, which allows him to move on to the *Washington Post,* where he is employed by the editors who have full knowledge of his time in prison. In the end, his original decision gives McCall a source of power: If his blackness provides white employers with an immediate way to marginalize him, he will not provide them with another. As he sees it, black people who venture into the mainstream for work already have to hide much of what is good about who they are in order to be considered employable by whites. He wants to be in control of particular information about himself so he can show his employers that things he did in the past do not have any bearing on his potential to become great in the future. Our pasts shape us; our interactions with people, our actions help us become who we are. But in McCall's view, these relations do not predict who we are to become; they serve only to inform us about where we have been as we decide what direction our lives will take.

Autobiographical manifestos are documents that present a view of the world from the margins, from the outside of the accepted norms and values. As a result, Sidonie Smith says, "the legitimacy of a new or alternative knowledge located in the experiences of the margins is affirmed."[7] As the autobiographical manifesto challenges the status quo, it presents the knowledge that comes from the experience of the marginalized. Instead of being looked upon as the product of an *inferior* experience, that knowledge is validated and asserted as the product of a *different* experience.

In examining the performance and announcement aspects of the autobiographical manifesto in connection with Nelson's *Volunteer Slavery* in chapter 2, I suggested that we ponder the questions *What is being announced or performed?* and *How is the announcement or performance being done?* in order to consider the content of autobiographical manifesto announcements. In that regard, what McCall's autobiography announces stems from a connection between the personal and sociopolitical. *Makes Me Wanna Holler* is a text about survival in the midst of surveillance. Its announcement is this: To be a black man (or woman) in America is to be under constant observation. This is evidenced when McCall discusses his day-to-day experience in the newsroom at the *Virginian Pilot-Leger Star:*

> As I stood and walked across the newsroom, I felt them again: the eyes. Like radar, they locked onto me from the moment I rose from my seat,

and remained fixed as I headed slowly to the file cabinets, where old news-paper clippings were kept. Returning to my desk, I looked straight ahead, pretending, as always, not to notice.

They weren't the evil, predatory gazes that I saw in prison. They were polite stares by curious white reporters, editors, and secretaries in the small office of the Portsmouth bureau, where I worked. . . . I began to get used to the stares. Well, I never really got used to them, but I resigned myself to the reality that someone always seemed to be watching, zeroing in on my every move.[8]

He provided another example from his time at the *Journal-Constitution:*

And then there was the black-male thing. I knew going into that news-room that there was additional pressure on brothers, but I didn't know it was that intense, especially from white men. I always caught them looking at us, I mean studying us from head to toe, checking out our demeanor, the clothes we wore, our shoes, and how we coordinated our colors. Some of the brothers dressed nicely in outfits that were appropriate yet stylish. Occasionally, one of the white guys would make a snide comment about the way we dressed, as if to suggest that we somehow lacked substance because we paid attention to our appearance. They'd say things like "I'll bet you spend a lot of money on clothes, don't you?" . . . They couldn't dress as sharp as the brothers and they felt insecure about it, so they tried to put us down. It was petty, but it was real.[9]

At the *Post*, McCall's feelings about being in a state of constant sur-veillance and hypersensitivity about black racial images are magnified after the arrest of D.C. mayor Marion Barry:

Barry's arrest affected me like many other disappointments involving blacks: Every time somebody black did some highly publicized evil or stupid thing, I cringed because I knew that, in white folks' eyes, it reflected badly on the whole race. Every time I heard news accounts of some drug bust, carjacking, robbery, or rape, I'd close my eyes and think, I hope it wasn't a black person who did it.

No matter how hard I fought, it was always there, that tendency to see us through the accusing eyes of whites.[10]

From McCall's perspective, African Americans are observed by whites and reobserved by themselves, seeing themselves through the gaze of the observer. Moreover, as the subject of surveillance, McCall acts as the observed as well as an observer himself of the actions of whites. In the end, he learns more than the whites who observe him, because in his view, white people look only for that which affirmed their negative assumptions about black people, whereas black people understand how whites act, think, and feel. This epitomizes how standpoint functions in ways beyond the mere theoretical, offering, as a result, a more inclusive view of society because it draws from the sociocultural location of the oppressed. The underlying assumption is that the oppressed have witnessed all the ways in which people on every sociocultural level operate. Fault lines become sites of experience and knowledge about the "totality" of the human experience that those who operate from a privileged perspective cannot access.

McCall, Manifesto, and Performance

It is characteristic of the performative aspect of the autobiographical manifesto to revel in the presentation of a "new" kind of subject. As an example of this, *Makes Me Wanna Holler* is a text in which the new kind of subject is that of the observer from the marginalized group who observes while working alongside the observer in the mainstream newsroom. For McCall, the performance takes the form of direct statements of his observations and italicized revelations of thoughts he does not express directly. An example of this is when he discusses how he interacts with the white reporters at the *Virginian Pilot-Leger Star:*

> There were always two conversations floating in my head when I interacted with whites. There was what I thought and what I said. Practically everything I said was calculated to counter some stereotype whites hold about blacks. If they brought up music, I responded in a way that said, Yes, we listen to more than boogie-woogie and the blues. Literature? Yes, I've read Hemingway, Fitzgerald, and all those other white motherfuckas you think are so good.
>
> They seldom knew what I really thought and felt about things, and I made sure they got few chances to find out.[11]

McCall also intersperses his life narrative with journal entries that reflect on key moments and issues in his life:

I have yet to grow accustomed to the free and easy nature of my job as a reporter. All my life, I've worked on jobs where white overseers stood close by and watched over my shoulders as I performed some menial, mindless task. They always were sure to make certain I never stole an extra minute or paused too long between strokes of the shovel. As a writer, I am now doing what I do best. It's difficult to believe.

June 5, 1981[12]

In his memoir, McCall becomes a knower who is not known. In his interactions with whites, he observes, records, but does not reveal his thoughts, except to the reader, who is then drafted into McCall's quest to carve out a private sphere for himself, away from the intrusive eyes of his white coworkers. But by putting his quest in autobiographical form, he robs himself of that private sphere, because the text becomes a document in the public sphere, where, as a result, it becomes a per-formance—one that seems to be staged for the very readers who are participants in his quest to create a private sphere for himself.

The performative nature of McCall's *Makes Me Wanna Holler* does not diminish his effectiveness in speaking as a member of a group. Writers of autobiographical manifesto adhere to group identity and eschew "radical individuality." For McCall, that identity is indicated in his choice of subtitle: *A Young Black Man in America.* He is writing, of course, as a member of a group and speaking as one whose experiences are personal, but are also, in a general sense, representative of the group. This is indicated by the double-voiced nature of *Makes Me Wanna Holler.* In the examples presented earlier as part of the discussion of announcement and performance, we see how McCall describes experience directly on the one hand, but how, conversely, the use of journal entries and italicized statements of McCall's thoughts allow him to speak to the reader *indirectly.* He speaks as one of a group and as an individual. It allows for two levels of standpoint critique of white culture.

Race is, of course, central to the identity from and for which McCall speaks. But while Nelson takes great care to make sure we understand that she is a "race woman," McCall does not make a statement of his racial identity. He is a "young black man in America" and, in terms of Aída Hurtado's concept of "relative positionality," has a much closer position to the dominant white male patriarchy because of his gender. However, to oversimplify the power dynamic in that way is, as Ellis Cose states, "to miss all the complexity and subtlety of the real world."[13]

As a member of a marginalized group and in his interactions as an individual, McCall has shifting levels of access to the kinds of agency enjoyed by whites.

One of the key themes of McCall's text is the idea of frustration. Throughout *Makes Me Wanna Holler*, McCall shows his disdain for whites and his anger about the impact of racism on blacks using pointed observations and criticisms of American society (both black and white) and the newsroom culture. From this, readers get the sense that McCall sees American culture as so tainted by racism as to be unredeemable without a complete overthrow of the system. However, it is McCall's interactions with Danny Baum, a Jewish reporter who befriends him during his time at the *Atlanta Journal-Constitution*, that help McCall to begin to think differently about his personal interactions with other whites in the newsroom and the frustrations he feels as a black person in America. Baum invites McCall to dinner at his home, and he accepts, an important step in McCall's personal growth. He writes,

> Thinking about it, even *considering* spending my free time at a white person's house was a major leap for me. Had it been anyone else I wouldn't have had to think about it at all. I'd have declined without blinking an eye. But I considered it with Danny and decided, *What the hell, I'll give it a try.*[14]

McCall is able to set aside his distrust in order to enjoy an evening with Baum and his girlfriend, who is also a journalist. During his visit, they share their views on books, music, and race. At the end of the evening, McCall is surprised that he spent an evening with whites and enjoyed himself. In return, he invites Baum and his girlfriend to his home. "It was the first time I'd had any white people over to my house," he writes.[15] It is during a Saturday morning outing that a question from Baum about being angry causes McCall to vent his frustrations about what it means to be black in America:

> "Race affects every facet of my life, man. I can't get past race because white folks won't let me get past it. They remind me of it everywhere I go. Every time I step in an elevator and a white woman bunches up in the corner like she thinks I wanna rape her, I'm forced to think about it. Every time I walk into stores, the suspicious looks in white shopkeepers' eyes make me think about it. Every time I walk past whites sitting in their cars, I hear the door locks clicking and I think about it. I can't get away from it man. I stay so mad all the time because I'm forced to spend so much time and

energy reacting to race. I hate it. It wearies me. But there's no escape, man. No escape."[16]

After venting his frustrations, McCall realizes that he has spent a great portion of his life reacting to what white people think, despite the fact that he had told himself otherwise. And he is quite surprised that Baum, a white person, is actually interested in what he thinks and tries to understand. McCall says, "[H]e helped me see the world through white eyes and helped me better understand the fear and ignorance behind prejudice."[17] Furthermore, what he learns from Baum is that even the most educated, well-meaning whites know little about black people: "Even though he saw us every day and interacted with us, we were still puzzles to him."[18] This leads McCall to conclude that the education system has failed whites more than it his failed everyone else. He concludes:

> It has crippled them and limited their humanity. They're the ones who need to know the most about everybody because they're the ones running the country. They've been taught so little about anybody other than white people that they can't understand even when they try.[19]

This statement allows him to suggest the future possibility of cultural change and racial understanding and reconciliation: the kind of education that brings understanding as a result of sincere and open-minded personal interaction, that allows for the understanding of different standpoints. On McCall's part, perhaps it is somewhat naive to think that understanding on a personal level can undo the pervasive effects of racism on black men, but it is a way to start.

By the end of *Makes Me Wanna Holler*, McCall is less angry than he is frustrated by the state of black men in American society. He returns to his hometown and sees that violence is pervasive, that many of his old associates have become part of what he calls "black America's running tragedy."[20] However, he has no real idea about how to address the problem. In his old friends and acquaintances, he sees how much he has progressed, and he understands what they are going through. He also understands that the simple reasons for their situations—the "convenient theories" of broken homes, misplaced values, and poverty—do not necessarily fit. He came from a working-class family and fell into the same trap, and he was lucky to escape. But overall, he feels that the problems that plague his hometown companions and many other young black men are "more complex than something we can throw jobs, social programs, or more policemen at."[21]

Part of McCall's frustration stems from the fact that he has developed a complex belief system:

> I have come to believe two things that might seem contradictory: Some of our worst childhood fears were true—the establishment is teeming with racism. Yet I also believe that whites are as befuddled about race as we are, and they're as scared of us as we are of them. Many of them are seeking solutions, just like us.
>
> I am torn by a different kind of anger now. I resent suggestions that blacks enjoy being "righteous victims." And when people ask, "What is wrong with black men?," it makes me want to lash out. When I hear that question, I am reminded of something that Malcolm X once said: "I have no mercy or compassion in me for a society that will crush people and then penalize them for not being able to stand up under the weight."[22]

When McCall speaks to the future, he cannot give "pithy social formulas" that will solve problems. But he fails to realize that he does not need to. The fact that he has appropriated a space in which to tell his story, and, as a result, become an example of one solution to the problem is, in the end, the best anyone can ask.

Nellie McKay and others speak of black maleness as a privileged position in terms of power; however, the "black" part of the position is still a fault line that is useful for standpoint analysis. Not as insecure as Nelson in his racial identity from a declarative standpoint, McCall speaks from the vantage point of one who is affected by the ways in which race is "enforced" in America and some of its more pernicious effects on black men who live in an environment that is detrimental to their development. Racism can hinder moral development and limit—sometimes cripple—the ability to make morally responsible choices. It takes powerful, transformative experiences to overcome the effects of racism. The effects of male gender privilege coupled with racism are especially damaging. As Maurice Wallace contends, "the structuring structure of the black masculine is neither a fully cohesive construction nor an entirely innocent one either."[23] It is not fully cohesive because it has never been allowed to be defined on its own terms; it has been defined on terms formulated by and in opposition to white masculinity. It is not entirely innocent because there has been at least a limited acceptance of the terms of the definition by black men.

This is true of the black male identity that McCall presents—and tries to define—in *Makes Me Wanna Holler*. In his youth, McCall was a black male oppressor who sexually preyed upon black women, and in his adult years has trouble dealing with women as equals. McCall is a victim of social forces that draw him inexorably into a life of crime, and eventually into prison, because in his youth he associated with other males who had neither the kind of emotional support system that would enable them to develop positive feelings about their potential nor a strong moral center from which to make socially acceptable life choices. For him, what being a man meant was defined by others who never had the terms of maleness defined in any kind of meaningful way. Moreover, if there is any power in maleness, it is a field of power that privileges white maleness in terms of the distribution of society's benefits. Still, even though the black masculine is still not a fully realized construction, McCall's memoir enables him to appropriate a position in which he has the power to attract the gaze of whites. His text is frank, sexual, and violent when it comes to describing his life. Sadly, by the end of the text, his voice is rendered less powerful when it comes to suggesting a means of leading other men who grow up in backgrounds like his, or worse than his, toward transformation. His voice is less equivocal when it comes to matters of class. Like Nelson, he seeks "authentic" black experiences, or at least *real* blacks, to balance out the "stone-cold assimilationists" and "handkerchief heads" whose existence he both disparages and pities. The son of working-class parents, McCall identifies with members of that class and with the lower-class men he describes as "hanging idly on street corners."[24]

The manifesto is a document rooted in the conflict between opposing sociopolitical forces. It records and responds to the promises made by a society and the keeping of those promises, its "promissory notes and their repayment."[25] The autobiographical manifesto documents and records the struggle by presenting a life lived in the center of the conflict. In *Makes Me Wanna Holler*, McCall has given us a document that not only presents a lived experience but also uses that experience to explore the effects of racism on the black male psyche.

Notes

1. Jill Nelson, "Makes Me Wanna Holler: A Young Black Man in America," book review, *Nation*, April 1994, 564.

2. Nathan McCall, *Makes Me Wanna Holler: A Young Black Man in America* (New York: Random House, 1994).

3. McCall, *Makes Me Wanna Holler*, 172.

4. Michel Foucault, *Discipline and Punish: The Birth of the Prison*, 2nd Vintage ed. (New York: Vintage Books, 1995), 200.

5. McCall, *Makes Me Wanna Holler*, 256.

6. McCall, *Makes Me Wanna Holler*, 256.

7. Sidonie Smith, "Autobiographical Manifestos," in *Women, Autobiography, Theory: A Reader*, ed. Sidonie Smith and Julia Watson, Wisconsin Studies in American Autobiography (Madison: University of Wisconsin Press, 1998), 436.

8. McCall, *Makes Me Wanna Holler*, 257.

9. McCall, *Makes Me Wanna Holler*, 300.

10. McCall, *Makes Me Wanna Holler*, 396.

11. McCall, *Makes Me Wanna Holler*, 261.

12. McCall, *Makes Me Wanna Holler*, 259.

13. Ellis Cose, *A Man's World: How Real Is Male Privilege—and How High Is Its Price?* (New York: HarperCollins, 1995), 12.

14. McCall, *Makes Me Wanna Holler*, 344.

15. McCall, *Makes Me Wanna Holler*, 345.

16. McCall, *Makes Me Wanna Holler*, 346.

17. McCall, *Makes Me Wanna Holler*, 347.

18. McCall, *Makes Me Wanna Holler*, 347.

19. McCall, *Makes Me Wanna Holler*, 347.

20. McCall, *Makes Me Wanna Holler*, 413.

21. McCall, *Makes Me Wanna Holler*, 413.

22. McCall, *Makes Me Wanna Holler*, 414.

23. Maurice O. Wallace, *Constructing the Black Masculine: Identity and Ideality in African American Men's Literature and Culture, 1775–1995* (Durham, NC: Duke University Press, 2002), 15.

24. McCall, *Makes Me Wanna Holler*, 372.

25. Janet Lyon, *Manifestoes: Provocations of the Modern* (Ithaca, NY: Cornell University Press, 1999), 8.

5

Jake Lamar, Patricia Raybon, and the Autobiographical Manifesto Form

I HAVE STATED PREVIOUSLY THAT an important premise of standpoint theory is the idea that because knowledge has a variety of social contexts, one can maximize objectivity by taking into account these perspectives. This suggests that we must redefine objectivity to take into account the "socially situated nature" of knowledge.[1] To do so means coming to terms with the possibility that biases cannot be eliminated. The result, however, would be a journalism that takes into consideration multiple subjectivities in its reporting. In that regard, I originally planned to take on the task of uncovering the role of memory and evaluating it in relation to the journalist's notion of objectivity and balance in connection with those limited subjectivities. However, exploration of the sociopolitical nature of autobiographical texts in question has proven to be more fertile ground from an analytical perspective. But Jake Lamar's 1991 memoir *Bourgeois Blues: An American Memoir* cannot be completely discussed without revisiting the idea of truth and memory, however briefly, in relation to the autobiographical manifesto's constituent aspects. I stated earlier that for the journalist, truth is fluid and uncertain as an objective concept. It is molded and shaped by the materials collected from experience. Through collection of facts and recollection of those facts, reporters arrive at the journalistic truth. Memory serves as the source text for journalists and autobiographers. In addition to using collected information, reporters often rely on the memories of sources for information in the context of their reporting. Autobiographers rely on the memory of their own experiences in presenting their life stories. As a result, the journalist as autobiographer is as much an artist as the autobiographer. The journalist as journalist, however, still has a responsibility to report reality. Unfortunately, this responsibility has not stopped journalists from promulgating fiction as journalism, as in the examples of *Boston Globe* columnist Mike Barnicle, *Washington Post* reporter Janet Cooke, and *New York Times* reporters Stephen Glass and Jayson Blair. This calls into question the nature of autobiographical truth when it comes from journalists. Since they traffic in collected fact and memory-based fact, do journalist-autobiographers have any more or less responsibility than other autobiographers to the truth? Simply put, an autobiography is what it is—the true recollection of a life lived during a particular moment in time—until stated otherwise. Autobiographies, as John Sturrock says, serve as the story of how their writers acquired the singular impulse—the focus and the conviction—that drove them to write. [2] Because we know this, there has to be some assumption of trust between the reader and the writer when reading autobiography. We have to trust that the writer's conviction that his or her life is unique enough to write about necessitates that he or she present the truth.

Announcment and Appropriation of Sovereignty in Bourgeois Blues

With this in mind, let us consider Lamar's memoir. In *Bourgeois Blues*, the announcement aspect of autobiographical manifesto transcends that aspect in McCall's and Neslon's texts. For them, the announcement aspect of their manifestos is a subtle feature, so much so that it can be (and has been in this discussion) linked to the performance aspect. As they perform race, they announce their frustrations with the kind of sociopsychological gymnastics in which blacks and whites in America are forced to participate because of racism. Lamar announces immediately that his is a memory piece—about race, of course, but still a memory piece: "This book is neither fiction nor journalism, but a work of memory; and while subject to memory's vagaries, it is faithful to the stories I remember."[3] The announcement in *Bourgeois Blues* changes the nature of the autobiographical performance by making the text more of a reflection of the blues to which the title alludes. Characteristic of the blues are their "strong autobiographical nature, their intense personal passion, chaos and loneliness."[4] Lamar's text is, of course, autobiographical, but by warning readers about "memory's vagaries" he allows himself the liberty of making his work improvisational as well.

However, Jake Lamar is not on a quest for a new self. His text is his way of speaking out against forces in his personal and professional lives that seek to tear down the old self and restructure it into a society-approved new self. His narrative follows a chronological sequence, but he has allowed himself the freedom to change the names of the people in his story, even though he describes their attributes in detail. Whereas Nelson and McCall seem to revel in naming people who are central to their stories, Lamar is content to omit their names entirely. For him, it is people's actions, their ways of being, that are essential to the formation of relational selves. In the *Time* newsroom, the person Lamar describes as the "quintessential company man" is "Player"; "Lifer" is the "dapper, middle-aged senior editor" and "representative of the breed" of editorial staffers who "shouldered a large degree of responsibility and made fine salaries" but who "occupied a precarious position in the corporate pyramid of fear."[5] Other characters include "Managing Editor," who instilled fear in Lifer types; "Baron," "a short, obese man with heavy-lidded eyes, a dense Bavarian accent and a taste for long, thin, brown cigarettes," who is editor in chief and the figure at the top of the food chain, and who relishes encouraging—and then dismissing—ideas from his subordinates.[6] With all their contradictions and conflicting character traits, the characters represent the kind of oppositional forces that form the standpoint Lamar's text is an explication of and a reaction against—but he is only dimly visible to them.

Lamar rounds out his cast of newsroom characters with "Minuteman," the associate editor considered a wunderkind by some at the magazine because of his extensive knowledge of American politics, his workaholic attitude, and his uncanny judgment; "Whiteshirt," the chief Nation section editor famous for his "deft hand with copy, his diplomatic expertise in dealing with his colleagues and his unflappability under pressure." The final character is "Survivor," the magazine's Chicago bureau chief and star black correspondent, who began his career as a reporter for an underground newspaper in the late 1960s. He serves as a sort of mentor to Lamar.[7] Even though Lamar does not give the characters' real names, he does not make them abstractions either. They are real men whose actions and reactions to Lamar help shape him as a journalist and enable him to write a text that is free from the rancor that permeates Nelson's and McCall's books.

Lamar appropriates the same type of sovereignty in *Bourgeois Blues* that other journalist-autobiographers of color do—by using the sanctioned space autobiography has supplied for African Americans. By adopting the sovereignty of the autobiographical space, Lamar is able to critique first the oppressive male sovereignty of the father with whom he has a troubled, distant relationship, and later the oppressive white male sovereignty of the *Time* magazine newsroom. In this way, he can critique from the position of the dispossessed and the powerless and, in turn, can better interpret both positions.

After establishing sovereignty, Lamar makes manifest in *Bourgeois Blues* the idea that even the possession of what he calls "bourgeois credentials" do not always take away the sting of racism from unexpected sources. He relates an incident with the parents of Deborah, "the coltish, quick-witted woman" he fell in love with during his first weeks at *Time*, while she was working in New York:

> I knew Deborah's family fairly well. She once told me that her father, a successful lawyer, had been particularly fond of me. That was before I started going out with his daughter. When he learned of our relationship, he was angrier than Deborah had ever seen him. Her mother took a more pragmatic tack: "Just don't marry him," she said. I was shocked. Here were people who'd enjoyed my company in their home, who considered themselves open-minded liberals—yet, they'd turned against me overnight.[8]

The shock of racism from unexpected sources and the fact that even his Harvard education and his middle-class upbringing are not effective shields against it impinge upon Lamar's interactions with editors during his stint at *Time* magazine. He struggles with dealing with whites who view him as more of a curiosity than a man, while trying to maintain his ability to effectively convey his point of view as a reporter who, although middle-class, is black. It is debilitating and dehumanizing.

Unlike McCall and Nelson, Lamar does not automatically assume a group membership that enables him to define the kind of new subjectivity Sidonie Smith deems necessary for the autobiographical manifesto. Lamar's text is *An American Memoir*. It is an intensely personal story in which the focus is Lamar's attempt to come to grips with the conflicted nature of his relationship with his father. But that is not to say that Lamar is completely removed from all group identity and standpoint. There are class issues that need to be considered; he does not shy away from his middle-class upbringing. He is connected to Nelson in that way, despite the fact that he is more than a decade younger than she is. Moreover, there is also the fact that, like McCall, he is a black male, and, as a result, has a relational proximity to power that Nelson, being black and female, does not. But in the newsroom, these identities are subordinate to Lamar's racial identity. Middle-classness and maleness mean nothing when trying to interpret the slights Lamar has to deal with, such as Whiteshirt's distant attitude toward him:

> Though known for his friendliness, Whiteshirt barely acknowledged me during my first several months in Nation. I might receive, at most, a faint nod if we passed in the corridor. "He's just insecure 'cause he didn't get into Harvard," Minuteman said. "He only went to Penn." This hardly seemed like a reason to snub me; and besides, half the writers in the section had gone to Harvard and Whiteshirt was quite chummy with the others.[9]

In another incident, Lamar discovers that what was to be his first cover story—one that examined the forces that worked together to perpetuate poverty in the inner cities—has been indefinitely postponed by editorial fiat involving seemingly arbitrary concerns: the content of photos (the women and children in the photos didn't look "poor enough"), subject matter that was considered too depressing, and a "squeamishness about running too many black faces on the cover of *Time*."[10] The editors' vision, limited by their privileged sociocultural standpoint location, limits their views about black humanity. Their limited vision presents a limited—and ultimately—dangerous journalistic truth; it keeps readers from a full understanding of the complexity of black life, allowing them to hold on to pernicious stereotypes without challenging their beliefs.

Race, Gender, and Class Connections in Bourgeois Blues

To say that Lamar does not wear his race as boldly as Nelson and McCall would be to lessen the impact of his text. If anything, he is confident about his racial identity in a way that the other two are not. In his youth, he encountered questions about his racial identity—-about what it means to be black—questions he found difficult to answer: "How could I explain that being black was the most important thing in my life and, at the same time, not very important at all?"[11] For the most part, however, he is realistic about the advantages he has had as a member of the black middle class. He considers the suspicious glances from shop-keepers who thought he was going to rob them and the "stiff formality" of some white adults who were not used to interacting with black people "petty annoyances," saying,

> If anything, my race had been an advantage. Among a lot of white kids, blackness conferred an instant cool; they just assumed, by virtue of my being black, that I was hipper than they were. I sensed that, to many white adults, my being black was a sort of bonus—here was a kid who was smart, friendly *and* black. What a pleasant surprise it was to them! These were attitudes born of prejudice, of course, but it was a form of prejudice that did me no ostensible harm, and I took it in stride. I thought, in fact, that by simply being myself, I was helping to subvert stereotypes . . . . The trouble was . . . getting people to stop abstracting you, to stop turning you into a symbol, to stop asking you to explain.[12]

Being black, then, means to be constantly on display, to be constantly subjected to the panoptic gaze of white people, who often fail to consider black humanity and individuality, instead focusing only on the "skin" part of the "skin you're in." But if one is constantly on display, it is a display limited in the ways that displays are, in that the observer sees only an object; it is a restricted vision. However, the object, though trapped, is also observing, positioned in a sociocultural location that allows it to witness all the ways in which people on every sociocultural level operate. The underlying assumption of standpoint theory is that the oppressed have witnessed all the ways in which people on every sociocultural level operate.

Much of Lamar's memoir deals with his troubled relationship with his father. He spends a great deal of space trying to describe and define his father's behavior, trying to compete with him, trying to gain his affection, and trying to escape the grip of his demanding, belittling personality. "Most men are neither good fathers nor bad fathers, but rather, better or worse fathers at different times in their children's lives," Lamar writes.[13] His memoir attempts to delineate the times of good fatherhood and bad fatherhood. It is when he gets into the newsroom, as the youngest reporter ever hired at *Time*, that he discovers the true value of the harsh lessons he learned dealing with his father; because of those experiences, he is able to negotiate the power dynamics in the *Time* newsroom between himself and the editors he discusses in the book—all of them male, most of them white. As in McCall's *Makes Me Wanna Holler*, feelings of anger and frustration seem to reverberate throughout the text, suggesting that these themes are central to the modern autobiographies about the workplace written by African American men.

As indicated by the title, *Bourgeois Blues*, issues of class dominate the focus of Lamar's book. Unlike Nelson, who shared his middle-class background, his struggle is not so much about guilt over having lived a privileged life as it is about making sure that he knows he can be an authoritative reporter on the issues of concern to all African Americans. But his struggle against the machinations of the editors when trying to get them to report on black people by emphasizing perseverance over pathology leave him bitter. The emphasis on pathology wins out. In the final analysis, his connection to class privilege does not ameliorate the white privilege that suffuses a newsroom in indirect racism. It parallels the struggles that Nelson faced during her time at the *Washington Post*.

Speaking to the Future in *Bourgeois Blues*

To speak to the future is, perhaps, the key aspect of the autobiographical manifesto. Janet Lyon posits that "[t]he manifesto is . . . a genre that gives the appearance of being at once both word and deed, both threat and incipient action."[14] It is a genre poised to assert the need for and suggest the path for change. It is a genre focused squarely on a future that is different from the present, in positive ways. Ultimately, *Bourgeois Blues* fails in presenting this aspect of the autobiographical manifesto. The constant struggle to gain respect for his standpoint as a place from which to report builds up frustration in Lamar. As the section of the autobiography describing his newsroom experiences at *Time* ends, he offers up Survivor as his spokesperson for the future. Survivor, who has moved back to New York to become the magazine's first black senior editor, asks Jake to write a cover story on the black middle class. Jake refuses, bitterly expressing his disappointment about the ways in which racism has undermined the editorial process with regard to his stories. Survivor gives him some advice:

> "It's like I tell my two sons," Survivor said, putting his feet up on his desk. "Racism is there. Racism is always going to be there. Racism is like hurricanes. If you live in a place where there are hurricanes, you can sit around wringing your hands and crying about how the hurricanes are going to wipe you out, or you can take the proper precautions, fortify your house, take intelligent steps to defend yourself against the hurricanes."
>
> "Or," I said, "you can move."
>
> Survivor's eyes narrowed. "Well," he said quietly, "I know how you feel. But it's easy to just stand up and run away. Sometimes it takes more guts to stay and fight the good fight."[15]

Moreover, Survivor asks, "Where are you going to go where there *isn't* racism?"[16]

Where Nelson speaks to the future by looking inside herself and McCall is frustrated, nihilistic, but still somewhat hopeful about the future, Lamar—at least in this exchange with Survivor—leaves the reader with a pessimistic sense of the future. In the end, there is no future without racism. There is only the present, locked inextricably with the past. The autobiographical manifesto is a text that looks back, but "it also gestures forward in 'the affirmative positivity of its politics' to new spaces for subjectivity."[17] It is about affirming the future and defining new types of subjects. Because Lamar gives in to his pessimism and is unwilling to effect change in the newsroom, he fails to take advantage of the opportunity an autobiographical manifesto provides to suggest new ways to effect social change.

However, Lamar has stated that *Bourgeois Blues* is not so much about rebellion as it is about "the impulse to resist conforming."[18] It is a manifesto describing a different type of conflict, a conflict between the need to accommodate the demands of a society that seeks to define some of its members in ways that limit their humanity and the desire for those members to assert and define their individuality against it. The manifesto is a reflection of the personality of an author, whether speaking as individual or as a member of a group, and it "takes on as many styles as there are writers and speakers."[19] It is a fluid and dynamic form whose rules are its own. It attracts us as readers because of this fluidity and dynamism. But it must suggest a course of action. It must contest. It must require something of us, if only indirectly. Lamar's memoir tells us that for blacks the struggle in life is to try to maintain a unique self in the face of demands that one subsume one's individuality into the collective, white-defined mass consciousness that devalues black individuality and the cultural, historical, and social contexts in which that individuality was formed.

Raybon's *My First White Friend*: A Manifesto of Self-Discovery

Patricia Raybon's *My First White Friend: Confessions on Race, Love, and Forgiveness*, published in 1996, is a collection of connected essays dealing with the subject of race and forgiveness. Raybon began her career as an award-winning journalist for the *Denver Post*. *My First White Friend* is divided into two sections. The essays in the first section, titled "Race," examine the shifting meanings of race throughout Raybon's life. The section ends with an essay titled "Letter to My First White Friend," written as a thank-you to the white student who attempted to befriend Raybon in junior high school. The second section, "Forgiveness," examines forgiveness in the contexts of "Seeking," "Finding," and "Knowing." Section three of the book, "Love," provides essays showing how she has moved past her hatred of whites and toward forgiveness. Raybon's memoir about self-discovery—and its accompanying epiphanies—is ultimately a manifesto explicating a new politics of forgiveness.

Like Lamar's *Bourgeois Blues*, *My First White Friend* is brief. But it provides an appropriate example of the kinds of forms the memoir-manifesto can take. A manifesto is a reflection of the personality of an author, whether speaking as an individual or as a member of a group, and it "does not need to lean on anything else, demands no other text than itself."[20] It is a fluid and dynamic form whose rules are its own. It attracts us as readers because of this fluidity and dynamism. Raybon is a print journalist who discusses her experience as a teacher of journalism at the University of Colorado. Insofar as her attempt to project a voice that challenges the ancien régime's insistence upon an unchanging status quo, she accomplishes this task. Like Nelson, Raybon is on a quest for a new self. The ancien régime she challenges is her own. The result of her quest is the truest among the four texts in this study to the form of the autobiographical manifesto.

What Raybon brings to light in *My First White Friend* is how debilitating fear masquerading as hatred can be on the one who is impacted. It takes away real power. It hinders the ability to forgive, because one lives with the expectations that come with being a victim:

> I have power. But for a long time, I did not know it. Couldn't fathom it. Dared not to dream it.
> I was too busy being a victim.
> And you get good at that.
> There's a cloying sweetness to it. Playing the racial martyr and being angry and indignant. Even when you're not angry and indignant. It's just expected of you—by the world, and its assumption that a dark person carries that chip on the shoulder.[21]

In order to avoid being seduced by the power she feels succumbing to victimhood allows, she plans to fend off its temptations, to find new ways to be herself. She exposes the power that racism has in dehumanizing both victim and the victimized.

After having exposed her own failings and the dangerous effects of racism, Raybon announces the way in which she will "perform" her act of forgiveness. Her quest for forgiveness will come through the telling of stories. Because hers is an intensely personal journey—much more so than Nelson's, McCall's, or Lamar's—the method she uses for her performance is itself intensely personal. She tells stories, in the form of narrative essays, to counter the stories she has heard over the years about white people—stories that made her hate, that made her a victim. She writes:

> I knew the stories. I had heard them in childhood, at the knees of people I loved, in the presence of people I trusted. Terrible stories. Horror stories.
> White people murdered Emmett Till and Mack Charles Parker and Medgar Evers and Herbert Lee and the four little girls in the Birmingham Church. And white people had acquitted the guilty.
> And white people had killed 6 million Semites and enslaved 15 million blacks (and sacrificed 30 million more, some say, to make the passage) and they had broken 400 treaties and irradiated islands and deserts and seas and even people. And they had robbed treasures. And they had reduced by 9 million through death and disease and denial the Iroquois and the Mohawk and the Pequot and the Oneida and the Seneca and the Arapaho and the Navajo and the Cherokee and the Ute and the other

Indian populations in North America to a remnant now of barely 1 million. And white people had stolen land and wealth and ideas and music and inventions, and broken promises and backs and treaties and will, and white people had stolen hope.

And I hated white people for all of it.[22]

In order to begin the process of forgiveness, she declares, "I will tell some stories":

Storytelling is the best way I know to make my witness—then release forgiveness from the confines of theology and dogma and academia, and also from the tyranny of fear—then examine it for myself, then share the journey with ordinary people: all of us, as we are, naked and waiting.[23]

Implicit in the declaration of her desire to tell some stories is the belief that by telling her story, she tells the story of everyone. Donald Polkinghorne has stated that narratives are *the* most important means by which people make their experiences meaningful.[24] We make meaning through stories. In autobiography, writers make meaning of their lives by telling the stories of their lives. Storytelling lies at the heart of the journalistic enterprise. But whereas Lamar, Nelson, and McCall are content to *report* experience, Raybon has such faith in the truth of her experience that she is able to make the leap beyond mere reporting to the *telling of stories*, albeit within the scope of what memory allows.

Raybon's *My First White Friend* is an intensely singular story. It explores not just the personal, but the internal. Because of this, the group membership characteristics that are more obvious in *Bourgeois Blues*, *Volunteer Slavery*, and *Makes Me Wanna Holler* are less apparent in Raybon's text. She does not position herself as a member of a nonhegemonic group or community in the same way that the other journalist-authors do. When she decries the ideology of victimhood, it is as if she wishes to escape the confining aspects of race. She wrestles with how to come to terms with the fact that race is a part of the fabric of American culture. Even near the end of her story, when she discusses her teaching at the University of Colorado, she bemoans the fact that "[t]he pressure to be black and immortal and acceptable" drove her and other blacks in the academy to set unreasonable agendas in the classroom.[25] This again shows the debilitating effects of privilege and racism on the victims: It pulls them down psychically, professionally, forcing them to push back against the pressure to be acceptable in ways that ultimately make them unacceptable.

However, if counter public spheres have multiple forms and get their power from the centering of subjects' identities around various experiences of oppression and exclusion from the central public sphere, Raybon could be seen as creating a *counter*-counter public sphere in which she is the only member. Here, she learns forgiveness of a sort. Moreover, she is reconnecting with an old literary tradition, for the most prominent feature of twentieth-century life narratives written by African American women is the authors' "rejection of black victim status in favor of a self-empowered black female self at the center of their identity."[26] By the time Raybon reflects on her experiences as a journalism instructor in her memoir, she has begun to do just that. Like Nelson, she situates her racial identity in a historical context, but instead of alluding to Nat Turner, she looks to the examples of Dr. Martin Luther King Jr. and his ideological forebear, Mahatma Gandhi, to find the path her racial identity will take. It is in these men that Raybon seeks the answer to the hardest of questions: "how to deal with institutional racism and injustice, not just the personal and the petty and the familial worries and insults."[27] From these flawed, human men she creates a self-empowered black female self, and she learns that forgiveness—the goal she seeks—is not something one feels, it is something one decides. The goal of the manifesto is to call to action. Raybon's call to action is a call for forgiveness.

Like Nelson, Raybon is a representative of that group of twentieth-century African American women who use their life writings to construct their identities from a standpoint that allows them to comment on a world that favors male privilege, white privilege. Moreover, Raybon critiques what she sees as the ultimate effect of the abuse of those privileges: the creation of victims both among the privileged and among the powerless, who, because they are afraid of losing the power that comes with being a victim or from victimizing, refuse to relinquish that power. She critiques it by deciding not to succumb to it, by deciding to forgive and work for forgiveness no matter what the challenges.

The fault line of class appears as an issue in *My First White Friend* as a means of highlighting the perniciousness of the hatred that caused Raybon to seek out forgiveness in the first place. Raybon lived a financially secure childhood in 1950s Colorado. Her mother involved her and her sister in organized activities that allowed her to associate with the children of Denver's black elite, but because of the racially charged atmosphere of the times, her "identity is never neutral," despite her middle-class lifestyle.[28] To the whites in Raybon's childhood memories, black people are still "oddities." And at the age of nine—a time in which the approval of others is paramount—she begins to develop the sense of rage against whites that would eventually lead her to seek to learn the value of forgiveness. Raybon's life stories are about how the power to forgive oneself and others transcends racial, gender, and class divisions.

Ultimately, it is what Raybon learns from teaching white students that helps her to affirm the future. She and her students have conquered their fears of each other, and in so doing, they learn that color "hadn't mattered for *everything*."[29] She writes, "That's the plain truth, and sometimes ordinary people need to remind ourselves: Most people are more alike than they are different. There is always, thus, a reason for hope. Even in racial times. Especially in hateful seasons."[30] With regard to forgiveness, she says, "Maybe I'm finally close to the truth—that forgiveness is surely fully impossible. You just work on it, and the working is what's good."[31] The autobiographical manifesto is a combative document; it is about conflict. It challenges the status quo of a society. In Raybon's memoir, we see that challenging the status quo to change means challenging oneself to change first.

Sturcture and the Autobiographical Manifesto

I have stated earlier that structure is important to the manifesto. Yet the fact that structure is important does not limit what a manifesto can be; we only know what they have been. Who is to say that the exploration of a life lived in conflict with society or with one's sense of self cannot impel us forward into action? Lamar's text allows us a different view, a new standpoint from which we can get a fuller view of the forces that compel people of color to conform to ways of seeing the world—of being in the world—with which they often do not agree. Raybon's memoir presents a standpoint that shows us the psychological effects of being trapped in an unprivileged standpoint and how sometimes the clearer, more complete view of society that emerges from being trapped in the unpriviledged standpoint is also a clearer, more complete view of one's own ways of being.

As I stated earlier, the claim of standpoint theory that knowledge emanates from diverse social contexts and perspectives should be considered as part of a journalism that replaces objectivity as a standard. It would offer a more inclusive view of society because it could draw information from the sociocultural location of the ignored. These limited subjectivities can be explored in the form of autobiography, as the form allows its writers to present the stories that explore journalism as the nexus at which the sociocultural categories of race, gender, class, and profession intersect. Journalism is a site for critique mainly because of its ability to empower people to effect change and its "comfort the afflicted, afflict the comfortable" ideals. If those who participate in the comforting of the afflicted become themselves subject to affliction by their biases, it calls into question the principles of journalism and the people who practice it.

Notes

1. Meenakshi Gigi Durham, "On the Relevance of Standpoint Epistemology to the Practice of Journalism: The Case for 'Strong Objectivity,'" *Communication Theory* 8, no. 2 (1998), 129.

2. John Sturrock, *The Language of Autobiography: Studies in the First Person Singular* (New York: Cambridge University Press, 1993), 14.

3. Jake Lamar, *Bourgeois Blues: An American Memoir* (New York: Summit Books, 1991), Author's Note.

4. Harry Shapiro, *Eric Clapton: Lost in the Blues* (New York: Da Capo Press, 1992), 13. The title of Lamar's book is taken from the song "The Bourgeois Blues" by Huddie Ledbetter, better known as Lead Belly.

5. Lamar, *Bourgeois Blues*, 112–19.

6. Lamar, *Bourgeois Blues*, 120.

7. Lamar, *Bourgeois Blues*, 124.

8. Lamar, *Bourgeois Blues*, 115.

9. Lamar, *Bourgeois Blues*, 125.

10. Lamar, *Bourgeois Blues*, 145.

11. Lamar, *Bourgeois Blues*, 83.

12. Lamar, *Bourgeois Blues*, 83.

13. Lamar, *Bourgeois Blues*, 35.

14. Janet Lyon, *Manifestoes: Provocations of the Modern* (Ithaca, NY: Cornell University Press, 1999), 14.

15. Lamar, *Bourgeois Blues*, 151.

16. Lamar, *Bourgeois Blues*, 151.

17. Sidonie Smith, "Autobiographical Manifestos," in *Women, Autobiography, Theory: A Reader*, ed. Sidonie Smith and Julia Watson, Wisconsin Studies in American Autobiography (Madison: University of Wisconsin Press, 1998), 438.

18. V. R. Peterson, "Jake Lamar: Standing Up to His Demons and Singing the 'Bourgeois Blues,'" book review, *Essence*, April 1992, 54.

19. Mary Ann Caws, *Manifesto: A Century of Isms* (Lincoln: University of Nebraska Press, 2001), xxviii.

20. Caws, *Manifesto*, , xxv.

21. Patricia Raybon, *My First White Friend: Confessions on Race, Love, and Forgiveness* (New York: Viking, 1996), 106.

22. Raybon, *My First White Friend*, 3–4.

In 1955 Emmett Till, a fourteen-year-old boy from Chicago, allegedly whistled at a white woman in a grocery store in Money, Mississippi. Three days later, two white men dragged him from his bed in the dead of night, beat him, and shot him in the head. His killers were arrested and charged with murder, but were both acquitted quickly by an all-white, all-male jury. PBS/WGBH, "The Murder of Emmett Till," *American Experience*, www.pbs.org/wgbh/amex/till/filmmore/index.html.

Mack Charles Parker, a twenty-three-year-old resident of Poplarville, Mississippi, was jailed for allegedly raping a white woman. On April 25, 1959, a white mob abducted Parker from his jail cell and murdered him. The FBI found his body floating in the Pearl River on May 4. FBI agents were able to identify the killers, but the state did not press charges. Timothy B. Tyson, *Radio Free Dixie: Robert F. Williams & the Roots of Black Power* (Chapel Hill: University of North Carolina Press, 1999), 143.

Medgar Evers was killed by an assassin's bullet on June 12, 1963. The accused killer, a white supremacist named Byron De La Beckwith, stood trial twice in the 1960s, but both trials ended in mistrial because the all-white juries could not reach a verdict. Beckwith was convicted in a third trial in 1994 and sentenced to life in prison. Melanie Peeples, "The Legacy of Medgar Evers," *All Things Considered*, National Public Radio, June 10, 2003, www.npr.org/display_pages/features/feature_1294360.html.

Herbert Lee, a farmer, was shot and killed in Liberty, Mississippi, on September 25, 1961, by E. H. Hurst. Hurst, a member of the state legislature, killed Lee because of his participation in voter registration activities in southwest Mississippi. Hurst was not charged with the crime. Charles M. Payne, *I've Got the Light of Freedom: The Organizing Tradition and the Mississippi Freedom Struggle* (Berkeley and Los Angeles: University of California Press, 1995).

Fourteen-year-old Denise McNair and thirteen-year-old Carole Robertson, Cynthia Wesley, and Addie Mae Collins were killed by a bomb set by Klu Klux Klansmen underneath the Sixteenth Street Baptist Church in Birmingham, Alabama, on September 15, 1963. Jonathan Rosenberg and Zachary Karabell,

Kennedy, Johnson, and the Quest for Justice: The Civil Rights Tapes (New York: Norton, 2003).

23. Raybon, *My First White Friend*, 13.

24. Donald Polkinghorne, *Narrative Knowing and the Human Sciences*, SUNY Series in Philosophy of the Social Sciences (Albany: State University of New York Press, 1988).

25. Raybon, *My First White Friend*, 202.

26. Nellie McKay, "The Narrative Self: Race, Politics, and Culture in Black American Women's Autobiography," in *Feminisms in the Academy*, ed. Domna C. Stanton and Abigail J. Stewart (Ann Arbor: University of Michigan Press, 1995), 100.

27. Raybon, *My First White Friend*, 138.

28. Raybon, *My First White Friend*, 41.

29. Raybon, *My First White Friend*, 210.

30. Raybon, *My First White Friend*, 210.

31. Raybon, *My First White Friend*, 226.

6

Memoir and the African American Newsroom Experience: Themes and Considerations

IN THE PRECEDING CHAPTERS, I have explored the function of the four autobiographical texts in relation to the public spheres, and analyzed the texts in relation to their autobiographical manifesto aspects. Here, I seek to examine what the autobiographies of Jill Nelson, Nathan McCall, Jake Lamar, and Patricia Raybon tell us about the newsroom culture and the "black experience" through their experiences in journalism. Four themes emerge from the texts that reflect the experiences of African Americans in the newsroom and the connection of that experience to the black experience overall: (1) the sin of being less than perfect, (2) the awarding of objectivity, (3) the devaluation of "blackness" as a point of view, and (4) the castration of the self/to be (black), or not to be (black). These themes show the importance of knowledge originating from different standpoints because they reveal the blind spots white journalists have that journalists of color must navigate.

The Sin of Being Less than Perfect

The sin of being less than perfect is connected to feelings of autonomy in the newsroom. The idea of autonomy is, as Carol Liebler states, "based on notions of control over one's own destiny."[1] In the workplace, that autonomy is characterized by having the freedom to schedule individual work and the ability to determine what procedures to use in making sure it gets done.[2] More important, it is connected to what Caryl Rivers calls the "Myth of the Incompetent Minority Worker," part of the army of unqualified minorities whom whites imagine as being hired instead of them.[3] In this concept, there is no autonomy: Whites feel they have no say in the hiring of such individuals, that they are imposed upon them without any consideration about the abilities and training of the new hires or their own biases and prejudices.

In Nelson's *Volunteer Slavery,* the "sin of being less than perfect" in the newsroom is described as "making a mistake," or, more specifically, "being wrong around white folks."[4] It is a concept that, according to Nelson, black reporters have to cope with as part of working in the corporate newsroom—one that has unjust implications beyond the newsroom. As she states,

> Not that there's anything inherently horrible about making a mistake, but when you're a Negro in America it's usually not just you who's making the mistake, it's y'all, the race, black folks in toto. One individual's fuck-up becomes yet another piece of evidence that affirmative action equals incompetence, that people of African descent somehow just don't fit in, that America cannot rely on spooks to do the right thing, no matter what Ossie Davis and Spike Lee say.[5]

Nelson's belief is exemplified by the case of Janet Cooke, whose imbroglio of journalistic ethics transgressions and the double standards applied to black and white journalists played out at the *Washington Post* just before Nelson is employed at the paper. Cooke fabricated a story that detailed the life of "Jimmy," an eight-year-old boy who had apparently become a victim of the drug trade that was destroying the low-income inner-city neighborhoods of Washington, D.C. Cooke detailed how Jimmy had become a heroin addict after being introduced to the drug by his mother's live-in boyfriend. As Pamela Newkirk notes, Cooke had written "the ultimate black dysfunction story, replete with broken English, teenage pregnancy, immorality, hopelessness, and a sweeping indictment of every law-abiding African American in the 'ghetto.'"[6] And for this, she was rewarded: In 1980 she won a Pulitzer Prize. However, the story turned out to be a fiction, and the Pulitzer was returned. Cooke's actions would do immense damage to journalism in general, and to the cause of African American journalists in particular. In addition, the reaction to the incident by the mainstream media, who roundly—albeit rightly—criticized Cooke's journalistic misdeed, also made manifest the "routinely employed double standard that allows whites, but not African Americans, to overcome egregious journalistic transgressions."[7] Newkirk says,

> It was as if Cooke—and blacks—had alone brought down the industry by breaching the ethical codes of journalism. The many transgressions by white journalists were instantly forgotten as the credentials of many black journalists were called into question, and their references and past employment were verified. Just as an individual black criminal was seen as representative of all blacks, so did Cooke's crime brand all black journalists.[8]

In reporting about dysfunction in a way that conformed to ideas that her middle-class and mostly—though not exclusively—white editors (Milton Coleman, Cooke's supervising editor, was black) had about black inner-city life, Cooke became the embodiment of the kind of thinking that Nelson says permeates the minds of whites in the corporate newsroom. It is a state of mind in which "[a]nything less than perfect behavior [by black workers] was construed as proof that as people of African descent we just never would fit in, didn't have the intellectual equipment to ever fully integrate into the corporate culture, were basically subversive, and thus should be viewed with suspicion."[9]

Cooke's fiasco at the *Post* reverberates in Nelson's autobiography when she discusses being reprimanded by Ben Bradlee for signing the initials of her supervising editor on a travel voucher: "He sits there giving me this theatrically intense scrutiny about a bullshit travel voucher whereas I'm convinced we both know the real deal is the discrimination complaint and any resemblance I might possibly have to his nemesis Janet Cooke."[10] In Nelson's view, her essentially minor transgression on a form for a trip that was preapproved by the editor who assigned the story is weighted the same as Cooke's breach of journalistic ethics by the white men who are her supervisors. Indeed, just as white journalists who commit breaches of journalistic ethics equivalent to Cooke's are not punished as harshly as Cooke was, as Newkirk posits, Nelson feels that the punishment she is given for her mistake—a week's suspension without pay—is greater than the punishments meted out to other reporters for even greater violations of newsroom policy, including plagiarism.[11]

In McCall's *Makes Me Wanna Holler*, the sin of being less than perfect is evidenced in his discussion of the "heavy burden" black reporters carry with them in the newsroom—"the burden of proving himself . . . constantly aware of that the slightest error in grammar, sentence structure, or story construction will be cited as undeniable proof of what white folks have always suspected."[12] McCall's assertions, like those of Nelson, are proof of the perverse side of the two-ness that is part of double consciousness. The burden McCall defines is the conflict between the "two warring ideals" Du Bois describes, a conflict that should not be taking place, but one that is inevitable when a person has to exist in a world he or she never made but must survive in.

McCall shows readers the ultimate fate that befalls a black reporter who cannot cope with the stress that double consciousness sometimes entails in the example of "Cassandra," the African American female reporter who began working at the *Atlanta Journal-Constitution* a year after he did. He reports:

> One day, she made a mistake in a story that required the paper to print a correction. Then Brenda Mooney, who ran the city desk, and the editor who supervised Cassandra made a big fuss about it, and after that, Cassandra's editor stopped giving her good assignments. She was given only lightweight stories, like weather reports. Sitting just a few seats away, I could see Cassandra begin to doubt herself. Every time she sat down at her computer to write, I saw her hands trembling on the keyboard and her eyes focused so intently on the screen that it looked like she was about to crack.
>
> Then Cassandra made another mistake in a story. I understood why. I understood that you can get so nervous about making a mistake, so tense about it, that it becomes a self-fulfilling prophecy. Cassandra's editor decided to get rid of her. I never heard her say it, but I saw it in the way she treated Cassandra. She put the freeze on her, giving her fewer and fewer story assignments. Some evenings, Cassandra would sit at her desk all day and not get a single assignment. I saw editors walk past her and get reporters who were busy on one story to work on another one when Cassandra could have done it.[13]

Eventually Cassandra's confidence was destroyed beyond her ability to recover. "She was a nervous wreck," McCall says, "fighting the myths and verifying them at the same time."[14] Giving up, Cassandra took a job for a smaller paper in another city, even though McCall said he believed that she still never fully recovered from the episode.

Neither Jake Lamar's *Bourgeois Blues* nor Patricia Raybon's *My First White Friend* deals with the sin of being less than perfect as directly as Nelson and McCall do. There is no overarching statement of what it means to be black or exploration of the "heavy burden" that black journalists shoulder in the newsroom. However, a parallel theme—the expectation of imperfection—emerges in their discussions of working as journalists, or, in Raybon's case, as a teacher of journalism. Unlike the sin of being less than perfect, which places the African American journalist in a state of near-paranoia about his or her actions, having to deal with another's expectation of imperfection often leaves the journalist powerless, with a sense that no matter how hard one works, negative expectations can never be overcome. In Lamar's book, the expectation of imperfection theme appears in a discussion of his interaction with the character he calls Whiteshirt, the chief editor of the Nation section of *Time* magazine:

> While Minuteman, Player and all the top editors had complimented my work, Whiteshirt was unimpressed. Reviewing one of the few foreign policy stories I'd written at that point, he criticized my saying that [Ronald] Reagan and one of his European counterparts had a "constructive dialogue." I had to admit it was a rather flat phrase. But for Whiteshirt, it had the most unsavory connotation. "Constructive dialogues," he said contemptuously, are what *Third World* diplomats at the U.N. have." Critiquing another story of mine, he said, "You seem to have a good understanding of the English language."
>
> Well, I thought to say, English *is* my first language, after all. But I said nothing. I just sat in my chair, choking back my anger. I felt completely powerless. I assumed that if I complained about Whiteshirt, I would simply be considered "paranoid" or "oversensitive." I could have asked for a transfer to another section; but that, I decided, would look like defeat. Besides, it had been more than eleven months since I'd joined Nation and there was a chance that, at the end of the year, I might be rotated to the back of the book. In the meantime, it seemed like the only thing I could do was to silently loathe Whiteshirt.[15]

Apparent in this passage, too, is the uncertain nature of interactions between white and black journalists in the newsroom. Even though other editors (all white) like Lamar's work, there is still one editor (also white) in a position of power who lacks respect for his work. To be sure, the editor Whiteshirt may have had the same disregard for other reporters on the staff, but it is the racial dynamic that makes Whiteshirt's interaction with Lamar problematic.

In Raybon's *My First White Friend*, the "expectation of imperfection" concept appears in the form of the topic that is both bête noire and topic du jour with regard to current-day discussions of race in America: affirmative action. On her first day as a journalism instructor at the University of Colorado after many years working as a journalist, Raybon stands in front of her classroom more than a little fearful of her students, thinking their exposure to writings by critics of affirmative action has tainted their attitudes:

> I expected, because they are white, most of them, that they would be indifferent to learning and also to me. I assumed that they had read D'Souza and Kimball and Bloom—and that they believed what they'd read. And I assumed that, because they were white, they wouldn't greet me with goodwill or, blessedly, even with neutrality. But with suspicion and fear.[16]

To cope with her fears about their expectations of her, Raybon tries to open up to them by allowing them to ask questions about her, but this leaves her feeling angry and defensive. Next, she tries comforting them. "I learned their names. I told them jokes. We laughed. I asked their histories," she states."[17] Still, the pressure of expectation of inferiority—of failure—feels"like a wet weight."[18] Consequently, she begins to feel that no matter what she does—"no matter how well or poorly"—whatever she does for them will never be enough.[19] Raybon is entangled in the constricting grip of "double consciousness." She sees herself via what she thinks are her students' expectations. But her negative assumptions about their expectations of her, coupled with her own belief that they might be true, are, in reality, her own creations; her students give her no real reason to believe they have made any assumptions at all about her, save for the fact that most of them are white. However, she associates their whiteness with the critics of affirmative action and the fact that whiteness allows for public critiques of black competence in the public sphere. The effect it has on Raybon is almost psychologically crippling, and this effect is exacerbated by the fact that "people were watching, then weighing" her performance. In order to cope with what she sees as the pressure to overachieve—to be seen as competent in the eyes of her colleagues—she overcompensates by overworking the students: "I worked those lovely white children so hard that first semester—fearful of not being enough for them, of living down to critics' low expectations of dark people like me—that I fairly killed them and myself as well. . . . And the students didn't deserve it. Neither did I."[20] For people of color, the quest to overconform to the expectations of others has a mental cost that victimizes the subject as well as those around them.

The Awarding of Objectivity

The second theme that underscores the experience of African American journalists in the newsroom concerns how objectivity is handled. As has been discussed earlier, objectivity as a constituent aspect of journalism is something of a chimera. Indeed, a roomful of journalists will have a roomful of different ideas of exactly what objectivity is. The fact that the Society of Professional Journalists dropped "objectivity" from its code of ethics in 1996 is, perhaps, indicative of how troublesome defining the term has become. Overall, as David Mindich states, "[o]bjectivity for journalists is often a question, not an answer—a point of debate, not a dogma."[21]

However, there still exists some expectation of fairness and objectivity among journalists. Otherwise, why would they still debate its existence and form? And there still exists an expectation of objectivity among readers of journalism who do not know how journalism is "done" or about its codes and changes to said codes. They only know that "objectivity" is supposed to be a news practice because journalists have told them so, even as they try to ignore its presence. Thus, "objectivity" will continue to live a shadowy existence, both needing to be explained and needing to be denied.

The autobiographies in this study were all written before the SPJ revised its code (though Raybon's was published in 1996). For this reason, it is possible to examine objectivity, as seen by the autobiographers in question as they provide an outlet for using standpoint epistemology to critique the ways in which objectivity is shaped by power relations.

Newkirk states that objectivity is awarded to blacks on a subjective basis. Black journalists "receive" acknowledgment of their objectivity only after they prove their ability to report on other blacks in ways that put them in a negative light or exploit them.[22] White journalists, on the other hand, do not have to be awarded objectivity. Moreover, they escape the burden that comes with being a journalist of color. How? Newkirk says that even though white journalists' objectivity is not questioned and they are presumed to be impartial, their racial biases escape detection mainly because "they ebb and flow with the tide of the news organization," while the viewpoints of African Americans and other minorities more often go against the tide.[23] "Objectivity" in journalism, then, is defined as being white, or more specifically, being white and male. As Nelson writes,

> If it's true that the only free press is the one you own, then it's not surprising that, at the *Washington Post* and elsewhere, objectivity is defined by the owners. Since those who run the post are white men, objectivity, far from being "independent of individual thought," is dependent upon their experience—sensible or not.[24]

The result is that for minority journalists, proving one's objectivity becomes the ultimate act of assimilation: proving one's white maleness. "A familiar means of accomplishing this is by writing a front-page piece that exposes, in great detail, the pathology of some element of the black community," Nelson says.[25] The Janet Cooke saga is an example of this act of assimilation taken to its ultimate extreme.

In *Makes Me Wanna Holler*, objectivity is not discussed as something to be awarded, nor is it something associated with whiteness. When writing about his stint at the *Virginian Pilot-Leger Star*, McCall states that what journalists are taught in college about objectivity does not match reality. They may start out trying to practice what they have been taught, but they quickly learn that "the exact opposite is true: journalists have feeling and opinions about *everything*."[26] For McCall, "objectivity" is something journalists "grow out of" as they become seasoned reporters. It is replaced by what he calls "professional restraint"—"the ability to swallow hard and hold one's peace in the face of people and situations that offend."[27] Professional restraint becomes a type of limited but privileged subjectivity that needs to be balanced out by other subjectivities in the newsroom.

When Lamar discusses objectivity and how it is performed in the pages of *Time* magazine's Nation section during the late 1980s, he provides the example of an editor he identifies as Minuteman, and his editing style:

> When it came to covering the news, Minuteman had only one concern: what was the "hot" issue? He had a nose for trends, catchphrases and

all things he considered new. "We only have to be right for one week," Minuteman liked to say. This he considered objective journalism. And, for *Time* magazine, it was. Because while the top editors made sure that a conservative slant went on most of Nation's political stories, Minuteman generally liked the articles he edited to have an on-the-one-hand-on-the-other-hand structure that at least implied impartiality.[28]

In the 1990s *Time*'s coverage of two racially charged stories concerning Nation of Islam leader Louis Farrakhan and the book *The Bell Curve* provide case studies about how "utterly subjective the awarding of neutrality is and how prominently race factors into that decision."[29] Newkirk notes that *Time* correspondent Sylvester Monroe was unable to get the kind of editorial support he needed to present to readers an objective portrait of Farrakhan, whose controversial comments about whites—particularly Jews—alienated some white magazine staff members. Ultimately, Monroe's attempt to present a neutral picture was undermined by his editors' dislike of Farrakhan. Newkirk says, "Monroe's attempt to present a balanced unfiltered portrait was overshadowed by intemperate headlines and captions that conveyed unequivocal abhorrence for Farrakhan and his views."[30]

However, the magazine's coverage of *The Bell Curve*, the 1994 book by Richard J. Herrnstein and Charles Murray that espoused the theory that blacks were genetically inferior and was supported by questionable research, received much more balanced, objective treatment. Newkirk says that such a treatment of the book was allowed because it reflected the white culture's own ideas about the status of blacks in the racial hierarchy.[31] These incidents were examples of how the media neglects to give black life the depth of coverage that reflects its complexity. Not having to be doubly conscious of blacks and members of other marginalized groups, members of the media tend to present only those aspects that conform to the views of the group in charge of the media: the predominantly white males, who bring to the newsroom biases that are developed in a culture replete with overt and inferential racism and sexism. By producing and reproducing media material that reflects the values of a culture that marginalizes people by race, reporters become part of a system in which they reinforce negative assumptions about those who are marginalized. When the information that emerges from a privileged standpoint is privileged without consideration of other standpoints, the "truth" becomes limited and inherently incomplete.

The Devaluation of "Blackness" as a Point of View

The case of Sylvester Monroe and his experiences with *Time* magazine illustrate the third theme reflected in the autobiographies of Nelson, McCall, and Lamar: the devaluation of the African American point of view in news coverage. According to Clint C. Wilson, Félix Gutiérrez, and Lena M. Chao,

> A common complaint of non-White reporters working in mainstream newsrooms is the application of unwritten policy to their stories and "news angle" ideas. Their ideas are often disregarded because White colleagues define news in terms of the dominant cultural perspective.[32]

Furthermore, Sherry Manzingo asserts that African American journalists feel pressured to conform to unwritten newsroom policies,[33] which they often learn about through content observation, editing by superiors, informal conversation, news-planning conferences, and sanctions for policy violations.[34]

In *Volunteer Slavery*, Nelson presents experiences that illustrate how her viewpoint was disregarded by her white superiors at the *Post*. Her autobiographical account of her newsroom experiences also shows how reporters learn about a paper's unwritten policies through editing of their work by superiors. Among the incidents she presents is the time she suggests a story idea to her editor about Oprah Winfrey, whose talk show was starting to become popular in the D.C. area at the time. Her editor, a white male who is familiar with neither Winfrey nor the local talk show host her burgeoning popularity is threatening to knock off the air, agrees to let Nelson work on the story. After the story is complete, it is transformed from a profile of Winfrey to a story about Winfrey's father, a change Nelson finds "weird, misogynistic, and dumb," but because she is trying to prove that she is a "team player," she does not complain.[35] After another editor—a white female—edits the story again, Nelson says that she barely recognizes it as the story she wrote. "The best I can say for it is that it's not offensive," she says.[36]

Another incident Nelson recalls concerns a story about Alton Maddox, the New York lawyer representing the victims of the Howard Beach attack.[37] This story leads to a conflict with reporter Juan Williams, whom she describes as "the perfect Negro, at least in the eyes of white folks, because most of the time he writes—and apparently believes—

what caucasians think black folks should feel and think, which is as they do."[38] The conflict arises when Williams reads the Alton Maddox story without Nelson's knowledge and tells her editor that the story should not be run—something Nelson finds out, to her surprise, when she goes to talk to the editor about the story. The editor says that the story will run despite Williams's misgivings because "[i]t's a good story," but Nelson is none too pleased about Williams's interference. This is significant because of the intra-racial power dynamics at work. Williams is the son of Panamanian immigrants, and to Nelson,

> [h]e typifies the worst stereotype of people of African descent who come to America inadvertently or willfully ignorant of the history of black folks born here. . . . These immigrants often have a hard time relating to and understanding African-Americans [sic], who after centuries of experience with what psychologist Na'im Akbar calls "the chains and images of psychological slavery," do not see America as so beneficent.[39]

In this instance, Williams is worse than a white person in that he lacks insight about blackness in America because he has not had the "authentic" experiences provided by being born black in America to black parents who were born in America.

Devaluation of black reporters' viewpoints is evident in McCall's autobiography when he discusses learning about restraint in the newsroom via an informal conversation with one of the black editors at the *Atlanta Journal-Constitution*:

> I'd completed a story and turned it in; then a white reporter made a lot of changes without discussing them with me. I got hot and went back and changed the story to its original form.
>
> When the black editor found about it, he pulled me aside and talked to me. "Hey, my man. Be cool. You can't lose your cool like that."
>
> But white reporters lost their cool all the time. Some white reporters, especially those considered stars and golden boys, went off on editors in front of everybody and it was routinely dismissed as mere temperament. But I couldn't get away with being temperamental. I'm a brother.[40]

For McCall, devaluation of his viewpoint is connected to control of his behavior, and a double standard imposed unfairly on black reporters, especially black male reporters. He learns that he must avoid being seen as a person with a "chip on his shoulder," because

[t]hat's the code for a phrase [whites] use when they want to get rid of black men: . . . They know they can get a response then, because no white person wants to run across a black man with a chip on his shoulder. They get images of Nat Turner, slave rebellions, and throat-slashing and shit. White men can throw tantrums in the workplace all day and night, and they're excused as "eccentric." But the second a brother shows some aggression, he's got a chip on his shoulder. He's *got* to go.[41]

Personal restraint is related to the idea of the sin of being less than perfect. For a black person in the newsroom, especially a male, to show emotion or react to a perceived slight is to summon forth in the minds of white people all the negative pathological behavior they have historically associated with blackness. Perhaps such a double standard contributes to Liebler's findings concerning minority men's feelings of autonomy in the newsroom: They felt less autonomy than any other group examined in her study—including minority women—and significantly less than journalists in the male nonminority category.[42]

It is the press' tendency to report on black pathology that is at the center of how Lamar's *Bourgeois Blues* presents the devaluation of the black viewpoint. Lamar is asked to contribute to a series of stories dealing with "race and poverty issues" for *Time* because, the editor tells him, "I think you could bring a vital point of view to these issues."[43] Though Lamar is skeptical, he is eager to work on stories that will "analyze the broad forces at work on the poor," so he agrees to participate on the project.[44] The reporters working on the series all send excellent pieces for the story, Lamar says, but after the series is completed, it is "postponed indefinitely," "a de facto death sentence" decided on by the magazine's top editors. Among the excuses given is that the story would be published too soon after an earlier cover story on teen pregnancy; other concerns about the article center around issues of race and the issue of poverty. To Lamar, it seems that a balanced approach to issues of race and poverty that goes beyond superficial pathological explanations challenged the editors' expectations and what they thought their readers expected.

In the end, all the newsroom behaviors described in the autobiographies are, at some level, examples of everyday newsroom practices that involve both minority and nonminority reporters. Stories get edited without discussion. Reporters and editors are unfriendly toward each other. Articles get shelved for trivial reasons. However, the fact that these incidents are discussed in autobiographies written by black journalists, and that these authors find the incidents so significant a part of their newsroom experiences, indicates that they are worthy of examination.

For Raybon, the journalist who became a teacher of journalism, her fear that her viewpoint would be devalued—a fear based on her own assumptions about her students' backgrounds—exacerbates her own feelings of inadequacy. Unlike the other authors, Raybon's position as a professor of journalism gives her a measure of autonomy over her situation. There is no newsroom culture to which she must conform; there are only the panoptic views of students and fellow faculty with which to cope. She copes with her situation by working herself and her students hard. Over time, she becomes convinced that the university where she teaches needs her viewpoint. Even though she says that her students are intelligent, well traveled, adventurous, "the invisible people of subcultures are often hidden from their bright eyes."[45] They need the point of view her difference provides. And because their blind spots concern her, she says, she is naive enough to believe that by simply being she provides a classroom presence that challenges them to reconsider stereotypical attitudes they may hold.[46] But she is affected as well, as they force her to look at her own attitudes: "In the end, all of us learn something from each other. My being here forces us each to cross a bridge and stretch. That is why I teach white students."[47] Her statement of epiphany becomes a declaration of purpose. By exploring a journalist's experiences in teaching, we learn the importance of standpoint and need for multiple perspectives in both the classroom and the newsroom.

The Castration of the Self/To Be (Black), or Not to Be (Black)

For African American journalists in the newsroom, the fear of being seen as less than perfect, the striving to be awarded objectivity, and the trying to avoid the devaluation of their points of view all intersect with the final theme presented in the texts: that of fitting in or selling out. At some level, survival in the mainstream newsroom—indeed, in corporate America—involves conforming one's identity to the expectations and norms of the corporate culture. For blacks and members of other under-represented groups, this often means conforming to norms they had no part in shaping. In the memoirs, the issue at stake is how much blackness to shed. In order to "earn" the same presumption of objectivity that white journalists take for granted, black reporters have to show a willingness to report unfavorably about their own communities. African American journalists, in essence, have to "perform" objectivity by reporting on pathology in African American communities in order to be granted the right to be thought of as objective. But doing so often means losing the trust of the people in the community about which you report.

Nelson says that "[t]oo often, if [black journalists] truly want to succeed and ascend, it behooves us to castrate ourselves in voice, demeanor, stance."[48] Those who are most successful at castration of themselves, she says, are those who "refashion" themselves in the image of white men in terms of education, clothes, and socializing. She provides the example of Janet Cooke, who "wanted nothing more than to succeed on white men's terms."[49] Cooke was "smart, pretty, had long hair, dressed appropriately, and socialized primarily with white people," and wanted to advance her career quickly, "like white boys do."[50] In the end, her desire to remake herself in the graven image of the white journalists with whom she competed led to—or magnified—"some severe ethical, moral, and psychological problems that lead her to mistake fiction for . . . self-hating journalism."[51] Ultimately, Nelson decides that she is unable—and unwilling—to fit in/sell out and, after checking the dictionary definitions of "resign" and "quit," decides to "quit" the *Post*.

During McCall's time at the *Atlanta Journal-Constitution*, he considers many of the black staff members who have fit in to the point of selling out "stone-cold assimilationists."[52] To him, they have given in so much in an attempt to please white coworkers that they have become alien. He says, "Racism was so painful for them that they denied its existence."[53] Their perspectives have become blinded. In trying to become acceptable, they marginalize themselves even further, as their standpoints become distant and blurred.

Even though he denigrates the blacks who try take a more assimilationist approach to working in the newsroom, McCall eventually decides that even though he knows he could never adjust fully to the mainstream, he thinks he might adapt easier if he conforms a little more, so he changes his voice, demeanor, and stance. But in the end, his attempt at fitting in fails because it does not feel natural to him. The shoes he wore then are relegated to a dark corner of his closet, next to the shoes he wore in prison. He says they serve "as a testament to the time I almost lost my way in the white mainstream."[54]

After the incident with the reporter named Cassandra, whose confidence is crushed by her editor after the paper has to print a correction for a story she wrote, McCall begins to feel sorry for the black reporters who try to fit in but are betrayed by the false promise that "if you make sure you are qualified, and if you assimilate and work twice as hard as white people, you can be anything you want to be."[55]

What Nathan McCall or Jill Nelson would think about Jake Lamar is difficult to say. He is, in fact, very much like the assimilated blacks they alternately scorn and pity. He's middle class and Harvard educated, and socializes with whites easily. But his memoir does not leave the impression that he has forgotten his blackness in the name of fitting in. While at *Time*, he remains vigilant against being used by editors to write stories that overplay pathology in the black community. He even stands up to an editor who disregards his idea for an angle on a story. Just like in McCall's text, Lamar's troubled relationship with his father—a self-made man who grew up in the Jim Crow–era South and abused his wife—is a central part of his memoir. In fact, Lamar credits the fact that he had to deal with his difficult father for making him able to handle conflicts with his editors. Unlike Nelson and McCall, however, Lamar has not set out to disparage the station of journalism. He is not trying to explore the contact zone of the newsroom in his slim book. His autobiography is an exploration of relational selves, of how personal, familial, and professional interactions shape lives, sending them into unexpected directions, sometimes with unintended results.

Patricia Raybon's book is also about a personal exploration of relational selves. She struggles with fitting in, but only within the context of interacting with her students. She is looking for the way to forgiveness. It is a personal quest, but along the way her story is shaped by her stories about others. Unlike the texts of Nelson, McCall, and Lamar, her story is not so much about a life in journalism as it is about the role of journalism in life. Ultimately, what all four texts do is map out the lives lived in the undiscovered country, the contact zones where the fault lines of race, class, and gender intersect in the newsroom.

Notes

1. Carol M. Liebler, "How Race and Gender Affect Journalists' Autonomy," *Newspaper Research Journal* 15, no. 3 (1994): 123.

2. Liebler, "Race and Gender," 123.

3. Caryl Rivers, *Slick Spins and Fractured Facts: How Cultural Myths Distort the News* (New York: Columbia University Press, 1996), 135.

4. Jill Nelson, *Volunteer Slavery: My Authentic Negro Experience* (New York, NY: Penguin, 1993).

5. Nelson, *Volunteer Slavery*, 149.

6. Pamela Newkirk, *Within the Veil: Black Journalists, White Media* (New York: New York University Press, 2000), 162.

7. Newkirk, *Within the Veil*, 162.

8. Newkirk, *Within the Veil*, 170.

9. Nelson, *Volunteer Slavery*, 150.

10. Nelson, *Volunteer Slavery*, 154.

11. Nelson writes, "The [Baltimore-Washington Newspaper] Guild unit files a grievance protesting my suspension, and digs up instances of a famous reporter 'losing' a rental car in a public garage for six weeks and being verbally reprimanded, a cub reporter making up a quote and being scolded over breakfast by Bradlee, a national reporter suspended for a week for plagiarizing." Nelson, *Volunteer Slavery*, 156.

12. Nathan McCall, *Makes Me Wanna Holler: A Young Black Man in America* (New York: Random House, 1994), 328.

13. McCall, *Makes Me Wanna Holler*, 328–29.

14. McCall, *Makes Me Wanna Holler*, 329.

15. Jake Lamar, *Bourgeois Blues: An American Memoir* (New York: Summit Books, 1991), 126.

16. Patricia Raybon, *My First White Friend: Confessions on Race, Love, and Forgiveness* (New York: Viking, 1996), 199. By the time Raybon began teaching at the University of Colorado in 1991, the anti–affirmative action, antidiversity critics Dinesh D'Souza, Roger Kimball, and Allan Bloom had books in which they denigrated cultural diversity in academic curricula and affirmative action efforts in faculty hiring in higher education. D'Souza's *Illiberal Education: The Politics of Race and Sex on Campus* was published in 1991, Kimball's *Tenured Radicals: How Politics Has Corrupted Our Higher Education* was published in 1990, and Bloom's *The Closing of the American Mind* was published in 1987.

17. Raybon, *My First White Friend*, 200.

18. Raybon, *My First White Friend*, 201.

19. Raybon, *My First White Friend*, 201.

20. Raybon, *My First White Friend*, 202.

21. David T. Z. Mindich, *Just the Facts: How "Objectivity" Came to Define American Journalism* (New York: New York University Press, 1998), 5.

22. Newkirk, *Within the Veil*, 158.

23. Newkirk, *Within the Veil*, 157.

24. Nelson, *Volunteer Slavery*, 86.

25. Nelson, *Volunteer Slavery*, 86.

26. McCall, *Makes Me Wanna Holler*, 266.

27. McCall, *Makes Me Wanna Holler*, 266.

28. Lamar, *Bourgeois Blues*, 124.

29. Newkirk, *Within the Veil*, 6.

30. Newkirk, *Within the Veil*, 6.

31. Newkirk, *Within the Veil*, 3.

32. Clint C. Wilson, Félix Gutiérrez, and Lena M. Chao, *Racism, Sexism, and the Media: The Rise of Class Communication in Multicultural America*, 3rd ed. (Thousand Oaks, CA: Sage, 2003).

33. Sherry Manzingo, "Minorities and Social Control in the Newsroom," in *Discourse and Discrimination*, ed. Geneva Smitherman and Teun Adrianus van Dijk (Detriot: Wayne State University Press, 1988), 128.

34. Wilson, Gutiérrez, and Chao, *Racism, Sexism, and the Media*, 128.

35. Nelson, *Volunteer Slavery*, 54.

36. Nelson, *Volunteer Slavery*, 93.

37. In the 1986 Howard Beach incident, white youths chased three black men from a diner into traffic, where one, Michael Griffith, was killed by a car. Daniel Massey, "Have You Heard? A Graduating Senior's Political Coming of Age," *Brown Alumni Magazine*, July/August 1998, http://www.brownalumni magazine.com/july/august_1998/have_you_heard.html.

38. Nelson, *Volunteer Slavery*, 90.

39. Nelson, *Volunteer Slavery*, 90.

40. McCall, *Makes Me Wanna Holler*, 302.

41. McCall, *Makes Me Wanna Holler*, 303.

42. Liebler, "Race and Gender," 127.

43. Lamar, *Bourgeois Blues*, 138.

44. Lamar, *Bourgeois Blues*, 142.

45. Raybon, *My First White Friend*, 208.

46. Raybon, *My First White Friend*, 208.

47. Raybon, *My First White Friend*, 208.

48. Nelson, *Volunteer Slavery*, 87.

49. Nelson, *Volunteer Slavery*, 87.

50. Nelson, *Volunteer Slavery*, 87.

51. Nelson, *Volunteer Slavery*, 87.

52. Nelson, *Volunteer Slavery*, 300–301.

53. Nelson, *Volunteer Slavery*, 300–301.

54. Nelson, *Volunteer Slavery*, 305.

55. McCall, *Makes Me Wanna Holler*, 329.

Conclusion

The Synergy between Race, Class, Gender, and Profession in African American Journalists' Autobiographies

THE AUTOBIOGRAPHICAL MANIFESTO IS A GENRE in which subjects either contest or appropriate a position of power in order to illuminate issues of concern through the announcement or performance of their life stories. The subjects accomplish this by speaking either as a member of a particular marginalized group or as a representative of that group. The autobiographical manifesto is a future-focused document; that is, it is a document in which the subject looks toward a future in which the issues that have been brought to light are addressed in a way that allows for the empowerment of the marginalized. Using myths and metaphors, they map out possible positive futures for the "individual" as a member of a group, so that in the end, whether or not the call to action is answered, the text provides us with hope by leaving us with the potential for "self-conscious and imaginative breaks in cultural repetitions of the universal subject."[1] Autobiography as manifesto suggests the possibility of new ways to break free from marginalization. It is "a revolutionary gesture poised against amnesia and its compulsory repetitions."[2] It is a genre that combats the promises a society makes and then forgets and the repetition of what Ida B. Wells in her antilynching campaign called the "old threadbare lies" that are used by the ancien régime to maintain privilege. The autobiographical manifesto does this by allowing for critiques of the various forces of oppression—social, psychological, economic, and political—at work in society. These critiques, or standpoint epistemologies, are, in the end, analyses of specific intersections of the aforementioned forces. They are ways of knowing how power is effected, both directly and indirectly, and how the use of power affects those who do have limited access to it.

Standpoint epistemologies suggest that there are multiple ways of seeing, multiple ways of looking at the confluences of power that lead to the marginalization of others. Because the autobiography seems to be the most inviting—the most democratic—of the literary genres, it can also be the most revolutionary. Autobiographies in general, and manifestos in particular, provide a means for members of marginalized publics to speak out from isolated standpoints and make their voices heard.

At their core, autobiographies are about individual experience, both in the living and in the creating of them. An autobiography is one person's story, even if the one person speaks for a group. This focus on the singularity of experience is what makes autobiographies worth studying; anyone can write someone's biography, but only one person can write his or her own life story because "only one person has the unique knowledge and unique access to it; only one person can also distort it in such revealing and mis-revealing ways. And only one person can speak about herself or himself in her or his own words, whether the words be kind or cruel, accurate or inaccurate, insightful or deceived."[3]

But autobiography is also a genre about group identity, especially for African American writers of memoir. This is the case because "the foremost concern of African American autobiographies has been the relation between the individual and the communal."[4] In African American autobiography, the individual life story has always been representative of something greater. The autobiographical self in the African American autobiography "is not an individual with a private career"; the African American autobiographical self is considered one of a marginalized social group who is connected to and responsible to the other members of that group.[5] African American life stories, then, do not exist solely as stories of rugged individuals who—in the American mythic tradition of rugged individualism—are clever and inventive, and defy the odds. They are political documents as well as cultural ones. They reflect a particular way of experiencing America for a group of people for whom perseverance is a fundamental means of survival.

The works of life writing in this study have been examined as quasi-political. My intent has been to show that they are documents that allow their authors to assume as well as confront sovereignty, and in doing so they allow their authors to address issues, they allow their authors to engage in an announcement/performance dynamic that enables them to take a stand for members of a group or speak as a member of a group, and they allow their authors to speak to the future. This makes the autobiography—in particular, the autobiographical manifesto—a document not only about lives lived but also about lives being lived and lives yet to be lived. As Jerome Bruner notes, "[A] life is created or constructed by the act of autobiography. It is a way of construing human experience—and of reconstruing it and resconstruing it until our breath or our pen fails us."[6] The goal of the manifesto is to stake out a position that will motivate its readers to take action that agitates the status quo. The goal of the autobiographical manifesto is to present a life that, in its presentation, will empower its readers to do the same.

A culture is a specific site of social activity. It is also a *specifying* site of such activity in which power relations shape interactions and replicate power inequities. Because of this, autobiography serves a unique role in delineating the ways in which the social relations in a culture affect individuals. According to Bruner, "An autobiography can be read not only as a personal expression, as a narrative expressing 'inner dynamics,' but also as a cultural product as well."[7] Moreover, he maintains that there is no such entity as a "true, correct, or even faithful autobiography," and that this should keep those who study autobiography from thinking too much about the supposed "self-deceptions" to which autobiographers are supposedly disposed.[8] So even when an author of autobiography warns readers—as Jake Lamar does—that his or her story is "subject to memory's vagaries," readers can be certain that what is in the life story is still enough of a reflection of the particular culture from which it emerges to inform us of the inner workings of that culture.

The autobiography, then, is one of the most effective platforms from which to engage in the kind of standpoint analysis that Nancy Hartsock maintains is essential to understanding the nature of power. For black Americans, the autobiography has maintained a special place in the discourse that provides critiques of power in the black public sphere. Lindon Barrett says, "African American autobiography stands as a peculiar site at which a critical reader can witness, in diverse realms, the dynamics animating fictions of the self."[9] African American autobiographies are evidence of the self-realization of people who manage to actualize themselves in spite of the social, political, and psychological factors that work to prevent their actualization. Studying American autobiographies, especially African American autobiographies, is a way of studying the problems of identity that arise from inequitable power relations, because the racial/cultural signifiers of African-Americanness are the result of asymmetrical power relations.

African American autobiographies are cultural products of significant value. They give form and shape to political commentary. Because of this, they are inherently political and part of the social spaces about African American social and political identity. Michael C. Dawson, however, maintains that there is no black public sphere of the type that Jürgen Habermas describes.[10] C. R. Squires concurs:

> Not every group or individual enjoys the same access to public spaces, media resources, or other tools to participate in discursive activities. Particular groups may be targeted by government officials for censorship and have a harder time distributing their ideas. Furthermore, prevailing social norms may instill fear in citizens of marginalized publics that their ideas would at best be met with indifference, and at worst violence. Thus the ideal of an open public sphere is difficult to realize for oppressed groups.[11]

If this is the case, then African American autobiographies—at least the ones written in the last twenty years—are at the very least part of a counter-public sphere that is still trying to find its form in a world where people have been relegated to demographic niches. To that end, the African American autobiography can be a significant and revolutionary voice with which authors can argue for the salience of their own realities without feeling restricted. African American journalists who turn to autobiography to express themselves wish to escape the restrictions imposed upon them in a profession in which they tell others' stories—those "others" include their audience, their sources, even their managers—while their own are not heard.

In their memoirs, Nelson, McCall, Lamar, and Raybon—in ways large and small—talk about the meaning of race and gender in the corporate mainstream newsroom, and their connection to the journalism profession. So there exists a synergy between the categories of race, class, gender, and profession in the authors' explorations of their experiences that makes the "whole" of their autobiographies greater than the sum of their individual discussions. In each of the texts, the author's presentation of the subjects of race, class, gender, and profession leaves the reader with more than just a story of one life lived, because each one acts, on some level, as an autobiographical manifesto. African American autobiographies are inherently autobiographical manifestos because of the always political—and sometimes politicized—nature of their historical origins. Because of this, they contain the most essential of the qualities of autobiographical manifestos: the appropriation or contestation of sovereignty. They all appropriate the sovereignty of the autobiographical form to show their lives in a quest for actualization, but the African American autobiography, as evidenced by the journalism autobiographies discussed in this study, may transcend the mere appropriation of form into other types of appropriation. For example, Nelson's *Volunteer Slavery* presents an author who appropriates the sovereignty of the single "authentic" self by contesting the sovereignty of the double-consciousness paradigm dictated by her middle-class upbringing. Being able to see the "other world" is not as important as being able to define one's *self*. Both Nelson and Raybon appropriate the sovereignty that arises out of a connection to other African American women who have written about their lives.

Moreover, McCall and Lamar, the male autobiographers, appropriate the sovereignty that comes from a connection to other African American men, such as Frederick Douglass, William Wells Brown, W. E. B. Du Bois, Malcolm X, and even Colin Powell. Their stories have historically been used for the purpose of providing the templates from which people come to understand black identities formed in conflict with white expectations of black identity.

All the autobiographers discussed here bring to light common themes that have made the post–Kerner Commission newsroom a problematic place for African Americans. They explore issues concerning performance, the practice of objectivity, the devaluation of African American viewpoints that differ from or critique the dominant viewpoint too directly, and interpersonal relations between black and white journalists. They make these themes manifest in a way that suggests a synergistic relationship between race, gender, class, and profession. In doing so, their texts represent both a public announcement and public performance. Nelson's and McCall's texts are the most performative because they share the intimate details about the authors' sexual experiences, inviting readers to see all the relational selves that they have.

Though the performances of the autobiographies are public, designed to be consumed by a mass audience through the autobiographical form, the voices in the autobiographies are intrinsically individual. The journalists share the group voice that is part of their shared experience of being black and American; their songs diverge. For Nelson, her text is "*My* Authentic Negro Experience," suggesting that *your* experience may be similar but not like hers. McCall, on the other hand, tells us he is "*A* Young Black Man in America," suggesting that his story is both like those of other "young black men" in America, but also different enough to be told. Furthermore, Lamar tells us his story is "*An* American Memoir," a generic statement that compels the reader to focus on the Americanness of the book's story. Finally, Raybon warns us that she is going to present, like Saint Augustine, "Confessions." She uses her text to discuss "Race, Love, and Forgiveness" in order to prepare readers to confront their own racist demons as they read about hers.

The texts all speak to the future. Nelson tells us that there are "authentic" black experiences that happen in the corporate newsroom, but that the most "authentic" experience a black person can have is being true to one's self. For McCall, the future is clouded by frustration, with problems too complex to be remedied with simple solutions. Lamar is frustrated and pessimistic about the future, seeing it as intractably connected to the past. Raybon, however, sees in herself and in her journalism students a way to create a better future by engaging in the ongoing struggle to move toward forgiveness of white racism and the effects it has on its victims. In final analysis, Raybon's *My First White Friend: Confessions on Race, Love, and Forgiveness* is the strongest of the autobiographical manifestos, presenting the most direct challenge to the hegemonic status quo or the ancien régime. For the individual to change the world outside, the revolution must begin within.

Journalism, as would be expected of any institution with lofty ideals, has created its own culture. The print journalism newsroom, for example, is a culture that reflects all of the qualities Richard Johnson says define the premises under which cultures are subject to critique. There are social relations within the newsroom that are "intimately connected" with the culture, including race, class, gender, generation, and geography.[12] These social relations also connect the newsroom culture to the citizens outside the newsroom culture, whom journalists serve. The second premise is that culture involves power relationships that create inequities in the ability of individuals to define their needs. In the newsroom, management/staff relations embody this type of power relationship.[13] The third premise is that culture is a place where social struggles and differences reside.[14] As evidenced in the autobiographies in this study, such is true of the newsroom.

The life stories written by Nelson, McCall, Lamar, and Raybon are symbolic of the types of experiences members of marginalized groups can expect to have when working as journalists in the newsroom. While they do not represent the complete scope of the African American journalism experience—and indeed, the authors' own experiences are highly individualized—enough similar themes emerge from their stories that they can be seen as representative of the African American journalism experience in many respects. Standpoint epistemology suggests that the sociocultural location of the marginalized provides a unique frame of reference for members of marginalized groups. From this frame of reference, observations about confluences of power in the social, political, and psychological arenas can be discussed.

Standpoint epistemology presupposes the idea that critiques about unbalanced power relations have sanctioned spaces from which to be distributed to the public at large, and that the public at large will be willing to hear the critiques, and, as a result, take the necessary action to address the inequality in power relations. Otherwise, the result of any standpoint critique is the proverbial "preaching to the choir." That being the case, in American society, journalism is in a unique position as perhaps the best site for standpoint critiques because of the First Amendment's protection of freedom of the press, which has been deemed essential to American democracy:

> The First Amendment provides the philosophical basis for democracy, because the reality is that communicating is the way we participate in the decision-making of self-government. As members of society impart their information, the public takes that information into account—agreeing or not—and the resulting public decisions are suitable to the greatest number of citizens. The more diverse information and opinions the public can hear and take into account, the more viable, more long-lasting the resulting decisions, and society is more peaceful and respectful.[15]

These ideas are reflected in what Meenakshi Gigi Durham says about the possibilities that could be realized if journalism took standpoint seriously: "Standpoint epistemology can advance the journalism craft by compelling journalists to rethink themselves and their craft from the position of the marginalized."[16] In its zeal to serve the market forces of capitalism, journalism sometimes forgets that it has a higher calling. It cannot serve two masters effectively. Indeed, market forces are currently killing the corporate newsroom. It faces challenges stemming from a decline in circulation, a decrease in ad revenue, and an increase in the use of the Internet as a means of getting news. As newspapers die off in print form, it is not clear what will replace them or whether that replacement will find itself obligated to present the kinds of viewpoints that allow for a more inclusive type of journalism that standpoint provides.

But attempts to get journalists to think about standpoint face a number of challenges on the interpersonal and professional levels, including making sure that other standpoints are valued. For the authors whose texts were included in this study, that was sometimes problematic because it often involved arguing with white editors about black reality in general, and their own reality in particular. This is why we must read and study the life stories of journalists from underrepresented groups. Their stories provide us with a more complete picture of the types of issues faced by journalists in their quest to inform, entertain, and enlighten citizens. Furthermore, these life stories offer a challenge to the status quo by illuminating the practices that hinder minority journalists from bringing their perspectives to the journalistic enterprise.

In the late twentieth-century newsrooms described by McCall and the other authors, the idea that there might be differing views of the nature of "reality" was a troublesome idea to some white journalists, many of whom were responsible for deciding what went into print. However, despite the frustration and unnaturalness of the arguments about what constitutes reality for which groups, the arguments must continue to take place—even if there are no winners. When those arguments stop, all citizens will lose.

Socrates said that an unexamined life is not worth living. We are unable to progress toward greater understanding of our true nature unless we take time to examine and reflect upon our lives. In the same vein, examining and reflecting upon the lives presented in journalism autobiographies enables journalism students and researchers to move toward a better understanding of the true nature of journalism. Ultimately, this will lead to a better experience of journalism for those who participate in its creation as well as for the citizens who depend on journalists to keep them informed about the world and, as a result, help them to examine and reflect upon their own lives.

Notes

1. Sidonie Smith, "Autobiographical Manifestos," in *Women, Autobiography, Theory: A Reader*, ed. Sidonie Smith and Julia Watson, Wisconsin Studies in American Autobiography (Madison: University of Wisconsin Press, 1998), 439.

2. Smith, "Autobiographical Manifestos," 438.

3. Robert F. Sayre, *American Lives: An Anthology of Autobiographical Writing*, Wisconsin Studies in American Autobiography (Madison: University of Wisconsin Press, 1994), 6.

4. Lindon Barrett, "Self-Knowledge, Law, and African American Autobiography: Lucy A. Delaney's 'From the Darkness Cometh the Light,'" in *The Culture of Autobiography: Constructions of Self-Representation*, ed. Robert Folkenflik, Irvine Studies in the Humanities (Stanford, CA: Stanford University Press, 1993), 105.

5. Barrett, "Self-Knowledge, Law, and African American Autobiography," 105.

6. Jerome Bruner, "The Autobiographical Process," in *The Culture of Autobiography: Constructions of Self-Representation*, ed. Robert Folkenflik, Irvine Studies in the Humanities (Stanford, CA: Stanford University Press, 1993), 38.

7. Bruner, "The Autobiographical Process," 39.

8. Bruner, "The Autobiographical Process," 39.

9. Barrett, "Self-Knowledge, Law, and African American Autobiography," 107.

10. Michael C. Dawson, "A Black Counterpublic? Economic Earthquakes, Racial Agenda(s), and Black Politics," in *The Black Public Sphere: A Public Culture Book*, ed. Black Public Sphere Collective, Black Literature and Culture (Chicago: University of Chicago Press, 1995), 201.

11. C. R. Squires, "Rethinking the Black Public Sphere: An Alternative Vocabulary for Multiple Public Spheres," *Communication Theory* 12, no. 4 (2002): 449.

12. Richard Johnson, "What Is Cultural Studies Anyway?" *Social Text* 6, no. 1 (1987): 38.

13. Johnson, "What Is Cultural Studies Anyway?" 38.

14. Johnson, "What Is Cultural Studies Anyway?" 38.

15. Donna Allen, "Women, Minorities & Freedom of the Press," *Newspaper Research Journal* 11 (1990): 12.

16. Meenakshi Gigi Durham, "On the Relevance of Standpoint Epistemology to the Practice of Journalism: The Case for 'Strong Objectivity,'" *Communication Theory* 8, no. 2 (1998): 134.

Appendix

An Annotated Bibliography of Selected Memoirs Written by African American Journalists and Broadcasters

Bass, Charlotta. *Forty Years: Memoirs from the Pages of a Newspaper.* Unpublished manuscript, Southern California Library for Social Studies and Research, Los Angeles, 1960. The unpublished manuscript of Bass's autobiography discusses her role as a peace, civil rights, and women's rights advocate. Bass, publisher of the *California Eagle* from 1912 to 1951, was active in political causes until her death in Los Angeles in 1969.

Blair, Jayson. *Burning Down My Masters' House: My Life at the New York Times.* Beverly Hills, CA: New Millennium Press, 2004. Blair's memoir opens with the collapse of his career. Then he takes the reader back to his early years in Columbia, Maryland, tracing his career from its beginning as an intern at the *Times* during his days at the University of Maryland. Along the way, he makes accusations, places blame, and shirks responsibility for the actions that lead to his dismissal from the paper.

Brownlee, Les. *Les Brownlee: The Autobiography of a Pioneering African-American Journalist.* Oak Park, IL: Marion Street Press, 2007. Brownlee—who, during a sixty-year career has worked for *Ebony* magazine and various Chicago media—was the first African American person to join Sigma Delta Chi, the fraternity that later became the Society of Professional Journalists. He became the first black person to work for a major Chicago newspaper when he started working for the *Chicago Daily News.* His memoir is a recollection of his experiences in urban reporting, his encounters with famous people, his successes and failures while working in the media, and how the media covers race.

Coates, Ta-Nehisi. *The Beautiful Struggle: A Father, Two Sons, and an Unlikely Road to Manhood*. New York: Spiegel & Grau, 2008. Coates, a blogger for TheAtlantic.com and a former staff writer for the *Village Voice* and *Time*, writes about his coming-of-age in Baltimore during the decline of the inner city and the rise of crack cocaine. Coates's memoir is a celebration of his father, a no-nonsense former Black Panther, whose tough-love style of parenting he credits for his successes.

Datcher, Michael. *Raising Fences: A Black Man's Love Story*. New York: Riverhead Books, 2001. Datcher's memoir deals with the psychological and social damage caused by an absentee father—in Datcher's case, compounded by his mother's abandonment. Datcher, a former editor in chief at *Image* magazine who also worked for the *Los Angeles Times* and the *Washington Post*, is now a poet and writer. The book provides a nonstereotypical coming-of-age and coming-into-success story of a young black man in late twentieth-century America, but could use a stronger, longer discussion of his career in journalism.

Davis, Frank Marshall, and John Edgar Tidwell. *Livin' the Blues: Memoirs of a Black Journalist and Poet*. Wisconsin Studies in American Autobiography. Madison: University of Wisconsin Press, 1992. Davis's autobiography details his youth in Arkansas City, and his years attending Friends University and later Kansas State. Edited by Tidwell, who also wrote the introduction, Davis's book chronicles his struggles against racial bias and his own negative self-image as he became a prominent journalist and poet in Chicago during the 1930s and 1940s. In 1948 he moved to Hawaii, virtually disappearing from the literary scene before his rediscovery in the 1960s. He died in 1987.

Dickerson, Debra J. *An American Story*. New York: Pantheon Books, 2000. Dickerson, a writer for *New Republic*, *U.S. News & World Report*, Salon.com, and other publications, can best be described as a political free agent. Her memoir is full of invective aimed not just at Democrats or Republicans, but also at African Americans, liberals, and the people she grew up with and met during her years as an air force officer, as a volunteer with the Democratic National Committee, and as a Harvard law student. Dickerson also submits her own ideas and choices to critical scrutiny. For instance, even though she was the daughter of former sharecroppers, she believed poverty was a choice; over the years, her politics changed from conservative to liberal to moderate. This makes her a complicated character who is most effective as a writer when she lets her stories, particularly those about her family, speak for themselves. More discussion of her newsroom experiences would add depth to the overall theme of the book.

Douglass, Frederick. *My Bondage and My Freedom*. New York: Miller Orton & Mulligan, 1855. This, the second version of Douglass's autobiography, contains a brief discussion of the establishment of the *North Star* in 1847.

Du Bois, W. E. B. *Dusk of Dawn: An Essay toward an Autobiography of a Race Concept*. New York: Harcourt Brace & Co., 1940. Included in this book's discussion of Du Bois's life is a discussion of his editorship of the publications leading up to the *Crisis*: the *Moon* and the *Horizon*.

Dyer, Joseph. *A Retired Black Television Broadcaster's Lifetime of Memories: From the Cotton Fields to CBS*. Bloomington, IN: 1stBooks, 2002. Dyer made Los Angeles history in April 1965 when he was hired as the first African American journalist by a Los Angeles network-owned-and-operated television station—KNXT (now KCBS-TV). Dyer's memoir discusses his struggles and successes at KNXT and focuses at length on his years at the station. It also discusses his early years working in Louisiana cotton fields alongside his uneducated, hearing-impaired, widowed mother. His book presents a clear picture of the racial landscape of the South during the 1940s, 1950s, and 1960s, especially the bitter racial confrontations that took place during the integration of schools and other public facilities.

Faulkner, Harris. *Breaking News: God Has a Plan: An Anchorwoman's Journey through Faith*. Leawood, KS: Leathers Publishing, 1999. A detailed account of the author's experience with a stalker—an ex-boyfriend who threatened her life—and how her religious faith helped her survive the ordeal and brought her a better understanding of why things happen the way they do. Provides an illuminating discussion of how she went from news gatherer to newsmaker and her reaction to it.

Gaines, Patrice. *Laughing in the Dark: From Colored Girl to Woman of Color—A Journey from Prison to Power*. New York: Crown, 1994. Gaines, a former *Washington Post* reporter, writes about her struggles in her quest to be a black woman in a world that values whiteness and maleness. By the time she turned twenty-one, Gaines was the mother of a baby girl and was in jail on drug charges. Her autobiography describes how she turned her life around to become a proud parent, an award-winning reporter, and a woman comfortable with her blackness. Her work at the *Washington Post* is discussed at the end of the book by way of describing how she overcame all the hardships and obstacles in her life. Nathan McCall, whose autobiography is analyzed in this study, is discussed as an example of a person whose similar background and position at the *Post* served as an inspiration to her.

Garvey, Marcus, Robert A. Hill, and Barbara Bair. *Marcus Garvey: Life and Lessons: A Centennial Companion to the Marcus Garvey and Universal Negro Improvement Association Papers.* Berkeley and Los Angeles: University of California Press, 1987. A collection of Garvey's works, including his serialized autobiography and a brief mention of his publication, *Negro World.*

Hobbs, Michael A. *Outcast: My Journey from the White House to Homelessness: An Autobiography.* Los Angeles: Middle Passage Press, 1996. Hobbs, who died of a stroke in May 2002, was a former *Philadelphia Inquirer* reporter who covered Philadelphia, Harrisburg, and Washington, D.C.; became homeless; and wrote a book about his experiences. His book, published in 1997, details his experiences after leaving the *Inquirer*, where he was a reporter from 1977 to 1983. As a general-assignment reporter for the *Inquirer*, Hobbs wrote about the homeless and homeless shelters. After leaving the *Inquirer*, Hobbs drifted across the country working for temp agencies before descending into depression, substance abuse, and homelessness. *Outcast* is rather thin on discussion of Hobbs's journalism experiences and is currently out of print, but it provides useful insight into the world of the homeless.

Hunter-Gault, Charlayne. *In My Place.* New York: Vintage Books, 1993. Hunter-Gault, a broadcast journalist with CNN, NPR, and PBS, was the first African American woman admitted to the University of Georgia. *In My Place* reflects on African American life in the 1940s and 1950s, the civil rights movement, and Gault's experiences at the University of Georgia, but does not include much discussion of her work as a journalist and how she uses her experiences in her work.

Ladd, Jerrold. *Out of the Madness: From the Projects to a Life of Hope.* New York: Warner Books, 1994. Ladd, a contributor to the *Dallas Morning News*, has penned a memoir that is an account that details his growing up in a crime-ridden, drug-infested housing project in Dallas and how he overcame the conflicts and struggles involved in growing up in this environment to become a success. Not much is discussed here about his work for the *Dallas Morning News*, but his focus on how he used self-education and determination to move beyond the circumstances of his upbringing is strong.

Lyles, Charlise. *Do I Dare Disturb the Universe? From the Projects to Prep School.* Boston: Faber & Faber, 1994. Lyles, formerly the religion writer for the *Dayton Daily News*, recounts her experience growing up in Cleveland, Ohio, where she attended the Cleveland Public Schools until ninth grade, when she transferred to the private Hawken School. This book contains no discussion of her work as a journalist.

Oliver, Kitty. *Multicolored Memories of a Black Southern Girl.* Lexington: University Press of Kentucky, 2001. Oliver, once on the staff of the *Miami Herald* and a former writer-in-residence at Florida Atlantic University, writes here about the struggles of her transition from the Jim Crow South to desegregation as well as the internal divisions and social distinctions within the black community. Oliver, who describes herself as an immigrant in an integrated America, has written a memoir that is also an upbeat journal of self-discovery. This well-written book discusses her experiences as one of the first black freshmen to attend the University of Florida, but does not contain much about her career in journalism.

Powers, Kemp. *The Shooting: A Memoir.* New York: Da Capo Press, 2004. When Powers was a fourteen-year-old boy living in Brooklyn, he accidentally shot his best friend while showing him a handgun. Even though the state of New York charged him with manslaughter, his friend's parents refused to prosecute. In this intense memoir, Powers, who went on to craft a career as a magazine journalist at publications including *Forbes, Newsweek,* and *Vibe,* digs deep into his psyche to discuss how that incident and his refusal to forgive himself affected his life.

Reynolds, Barbara A. *No, I Won't Shut Up: Thirty Years of Telling It Like It Is.* Temple Hills, MD: JFJ Publishing, 1998. Reynolds, a former member of the editorial board of *USA Today,* has written a quasi-autobiographical book composed of collected columns, commentaries, and sermons that show how she moved from a 1960s radical who once condemned the church, to columnist, to ordained minister. Provides a good discussion of positive effects of diversity and how and why the media promulgates negative images of blacks.

Richburg, Keith B. *Out of America: A Black Man Confronts Africa.* New York: BasicBooks, 1997. Richburg discusses his travels through Africa from Rwanda to Zaire while based in Nairobi as the Africa bureau chief for the *Washington Post.* Reflecting on his time in Africa, Richburg concludes that he is simply an American, not an African American. He candidly discusses his gratitude that his ancestors made it to America, while castigating Western whites who are afraid to blame Africa's woes on Africa's people, for fear of being called racist. He then criticizes white Americans whom he believes are afraid to hold black Americans responsible for their own woes. Less invective and more discussion of the newsroom activities would be make this book more insightful.

Rowan, Carl Thomas. *Breaking Barriers: A Memoir.* New York: Harper Perennial, 1992. In his autobiography, Rowan, an award-winning journalist who served in the Kennedy and Johnson administrations, provides a revealing account of his private and public life. From a poverty-stricken Depression childhood in Tennessee, he rose to become an influential journalist, and his memoir interweaves vivid eyewitness accounts of Martin Luther King Jr., the Little Rock protests, and other signposts of the civil rights movement. He also discusses his time as Deputy Assistant Secretary in the State Department and as American Ambassador to Finland. Most interesting are his discussions of the modern presidencies of Lyndon B. Johnson, Ronald Reagan, and George H. W. Bush, and his work as an independent syndicated columnist.

Schuyler, George Samuel. *Black and Conservative: The Autobiography of George S. Schuyler*. New Rochelle, NY: Arlington House, 1966. Schuyler worked for the black newspapers the *Messenger* and the *Pittsburgh Courier*, he was also friends with H. L. Mencken and contributed to the *American Mercury* when Mencken was the editor of that once-proud journal. Though he is probably best known for his satirical novels *Black No More* and *Black Empire*, his autobiography is worth reading for its detailed discussion of his journalistic work with the *Courier*.

Staples, Brent A. *Parallel Time: Growing up in Black and White*. New York: Pantheon Books, 1994. Staples, a member of the editorial board of the *New York Times*, recalls his hardscrabble boyhood in the mostly black world of Chester, Pennsylvania, and the pains and privileges that came along with later joining the middle class. The oldest son among nine children, Staples candidly reflects on his past and addresses questions of loyalty to his family, his race, and his class. Among the most interesting discussions in the book include his older sister's slipping toward delinquency, his being taunted by bullies at a new school, and the untimely shooting death of his cousin. The book ends with the first success of Staples's journalism career, which is paralleled with the death of his drug-dealing brother, Blake, in 1983.

Waters, Enoch P. *American Diary: A Personal History of the Black Press*. Chicago: Path Press, 1987. Waters's book outlines the history of the black press in America and recounts the author's experiences as a journalist. He also analyzes the attitudes of white journalists toward blacks and how those attitudes affect coverage of racial issues.

Wells-Barnett, Ida B., and Alfreda Duster. *Crusade for Justice: The Autobiography of Ida B. Wells*. Negro American Biographies and Autobiographies. Chicago: University of Chicago Press, 1972. Wells's autobiography, which was edited by her daughter, was first published in 1970. More a series of journal entries than a straight narrative, the book contains some discussion of her journalism work in Memphis, Tennessee, and on the *New York Age*.

Bibliography

Adams, Timothy Dow. *Telling Lies in Modern American Autobiography*. Chapel Hill: University of North Carolina Pres, 1990.

Allen, Donna. "Women, Minorities & Freedom of the Press." *Newspaper Research Journal* 11 (1990): 10–17.

American Society of Newspaper Editors. "Newsroom Employment Census." April 12, 2005. www.asne.org/index.cfm?id=5646.

———. "2001 ASNE Census Finds Newsrooms Less Diverse: Increased Hiring of Minorities Blunted by Departure Rate." Press release, April 3, 2001. www.asne.org/kiosk/diversity/2001Survey/2001CensusReport.htm.

Andrews, William L. *African American Autobiography: A Collection of Critical Essays*. New Century Views. Englewood Cliffs, NJ: Prentice Hall, 1993.

Baker, Houston A. "Theoretical Returns." In *African American Literary Theory: A Reader*, edited by Winston Napier, 421–42. New York: New York University Press, 2000.

Barrett, Lindon. "Self-Knowledge, Law, and African American Autobiography: Lucy A. Delaney's 'From the Darkness Cometh the Light.'" In *The Culture of Autobiography: Constructions of Self-Representation*, edited by Robert Folkenflik, 104–24. Irvine Studies in the Humanities. Stanford, CA: Stanford University Press, 1993.

Braxton, Joanne M. *Black Women Writing Autobiography: A Tradition within a Tradition*. Philadelphia: Temple University Press, 1989.

Bruner, Jerome. "The Autobiographical Process." In *The Culture of Autobiography: Constructions of Self-Representation*, edited by Robert Folkenflik, 38–56. Irvine Studies in the Humanities. Stanford, CA: Stanford University Press, 1993.

Caws, Mary Ann. *Manifesto: A Century of Isms.* Lincoln: University of Nebraska Press, 2001.

Collins, Patricia Hill. *Black Feminist Thought: Knowledge, Consciousness, and the Politics of Empowerment.* Rev. 10th anniversary ed. New York: Routledge, 2000.

Cose, Ellis. *A Man's World: How Real Is Male Privilege—and How High Is Its Price?* New York: HarperCollins, 1995.

———. *The Rage of a Privileged Class.* New York: HarperCollins, 1993.

Croteau, David, and William Hoynes. *Media/Society: Industries, Images, and Audiences.* 3rd ed. Thousand Oaks, CA: Pine Forge, 2003.

Dates, Jannette L., and Edward C. Pease. "Warping the World: Media's Mangled Images of Race." *Media Studies Journal* 8, no. 3 (1994): 89–96.

Dawson, Michael C. "A Black Counterpublic? Economic Earthquakes, Racial Agenda(s), and Black Politics." In *The Black Public Sphere: A Public Culture Book,* edited by Black Public Sphere Collective, 199–227. Black Literature and Culture. Chicago: University of Chicago Press, 1995.

Dickinson, Emily. "Tell All the Truth but Tell It Slant." In *The Norton Anthology of Poetry,* edited by Margaret W. Ferguson, Mary Jo Salter, and Jon Stallworthy, 1024. New York: W. W. Norton, 1996.

Du Bois, W. E. B. *The Souls of Black Folk.* Millwood, NY: Kraus-Thomson Organization, 1973.

Durham, Meenakshi Gigi. "On the Relevance of Standpoint Epistemology to the Practice of Journalism: The Case for 'Strong Objectivity.'" *Communication Theory* 8, no. 2 (1998): 117–40.

Eakin, Paul John. *How Our Lives Become Stories: Making Selves.* Cornell Paperbacks. Ithaca, NY: Cornell University Press, 1999.

Folkenflik, Robert. *The Culture of Autobiography: Constructions of Self-Representation.* Irvine Studies in the Humanities. Stanford, CA: Stanford University Press, 1993.

Foucault, Michel. *Discipline and Punish: The Birth of the Prison.* 2nd Vintage ed. New York: Vintage Books, 1995.

Fuller, Jack. *News Values: Ideas for an Information Age.* Chicago: University of Chicago Press, 1996.

Good, Howard. *The Journalist as Autobiographer.* Metuchen, NJ: Scarecrow Press, 1993.

Gross, Richard, Patricia A. Curtin, and Glen T. Cameron. "Diversity Advances Both Journalism, Business." *Newspaper Research Journal* 22, no. 2 (2001): 14–27.

Habermas, Jürgen. "Civil Society and the Political Public Sphere." In *Contemporary Sociological Theory,* edited by Craig J. Calhoun, 358–76. Blackwell Readers in Sociology. Oxford: Blackwell, 2002.

Hall, Stuart. "Cultural Identity and Diaspora." In *Identity: Community, Culture, Difference,* edited by Jonathan Rutherford, 222–37. London: Lawrence & Wishart, 1990.

———. "Minimal Selves." In *ICA Documents 6: Identity*, edited by Luisa Appignanesi, 44–46. London: Institute of Contemporary Arts, 1987.

Hampl, Patricia. "Memory and Imagination." In *The Fourth Genre: Contemporary Writers of/on Creative Nonfiction*, edited by Robert L. Root and Michael Steinberg, 259–68. New York: Longman, 2002.

Harding, Sandra G. *The Science Question in Feminism*. Ithaca, NY: Cornell University Press, 1986.

Hartley, John. *Communication, Cultural and Media Studies: The Key Concepts*. 3rd ed. Routledge Key Guides. London: Routledge, 2002.

Hartsock, Nancy C. M. "Foucault on Power: A Theory for Women." In *Feminism/Postmodernism*, edited by Linda J. Nicholson, 157–72. Thinking Gender. New York: Routledge, 1990.

———. *Money, Sex, and Power: Toward a Feminist Historical Materialism*. Longman Series in Feminist Theory. New York: Longman, 1983.

Hubbard, Lee. "Mainstream Newspapers Fade to White." May 1, 2001. http://lists.topica.com/lists/TheBlackList/read/message.html?sort=t&mid=1303992223.

Hurtado, Aída. *The Color of Privilege: Three Blasphemies on Race and Feminism*. Critical Perspectives on Women and Gender. Ann Arbor: University of Michigan Press, 1996.

Ives, Peter M. "The Whole Truth." In *The Fourth Genre: Contemporary Writers of/on Creative Nonfiction*, edited by Robert L. Root and Michael Steinberg, 269–76. New York: Longman, 2002.

Jaggar, Alison M. *Feminist Politics and Human Nature*. Philosophy and Society. Totowa, NJ: Rowman & Allanheld, 1983.

Johnson, Richard. "What Is Cultural Studies Anyway?" *Social Text* 6, no. 1 (1987): 38–80.

Kovach, Bill, and Tom Rosenstiel. *The Elements of Journalism: What Newspeople Should Know and the Public Should Expect*. New York: Crown, 2001.

Kupfer, Fern. "Everything but the Truth?" In *The Fourth Genre: Contemporary Writers of/on Creative Nonfiction*, edited by Robert L. Root and Michael Steinberg, 291–93. New York: Longman, 2002.

Lamar, Jake. *Bourgeois Blues: An American Memoir*. New York: Summit Books, 1991.

Lawrence, David. "Broken Ladders, Revolving Doors: The Need for Pluralism in the Newsroom." *Newspaper Research Journal* 11 (1990): 18–25.

Liebler, Carol M. "How Race and Gender Affect Journalists' Autonomy." *Newspaper Research Journal* 15, no. 3 (1994): 122–30.

Lyon, Janet. *Manifestoes: Provocations of the Modern*. Ithaca, NY: Cornell University Press, 1999.

Manzingo, Sherry. "Minorities and Social Control in the Newsroom." In *Discourse and Discrimination*, edited by Geneva Smitherman and Teun Adrianus van Dijk, 93–130. Detroit: Wayne State University Press, 1988.

Martin, P. Y. "'Mobilizing Masculinities': Women's Experiences of Men at Work." *Organization* 8, no. 4 (2001): 587–618.

Martindale, Carolyn. *The White Press and Black America.* Contributions in Afro-American and African Studies, no. 97. Westport, CT: Greenwood, 1986.

Marx, Karl, Friedrich Engels, and Robert C. Tucker. *The Marx-Engels Reader.* 2nd ed. New York: Norton, 1978.

Massey, Daniel. "Have You Heard? A Graduating Senior's Political Coming of Age." *Brown Alumni Magazine,* July/August 1988. www.brownalumnimagazine.com/july/august_1998/have_you_heard.html.

McCall, Nathan. *Makes Me Wanna Holler: A Young Black Man in America.* New York: Random House, 1994.

McGowan, William. *Coloring the News: How Crusading for Diversity Has Corrupted American Journalism.* San Francisco: Encounter Books, 2001.

McKay, Nellie. "The Narrative Self: Race, Politics, and Culture in Black American Women's Autobiography." In *Feminisms in the Academy,* edited by Domna C. Stanton and Abigail J. Stewart, 96–107. Ann Arbor: University of Michigan Press, 1995.

Mindich, David T. Z. *Just the Facts: How "Objectivity" Came to Define American Journalism.* New York: New York University Press, 1998.

Mostern, Kenneth. *Autobiography and Black Identity Politics: Racialization in Twentieth-Century America.* Cultural Margins, no. 7. New York: Cambridge University Press, 1999.

Nelson, Jill. "Makes Me Wanna Holler: A Young Black Man in America." Book review. *Nation,* April 1994, 562–66.

———. *Volunteer Slavery: My Authentic Negro Experience.* New York: Penguin, 1993.

Newkirk, Pamela. *Within the Veil: Black Journalists, White Media.* New York: New York University Press, 2000.

Orbe, Mark P. *Constructing Co-Cultural Theory: An Explication of Culture, Power, and Communication,* 159. Thousand Oaks, CA: Sage, 1998.

Payne, Charles M. *I've Got the Light of Freedom: The Organizing Tradition and the Mississippi Freedom Struggle.* Berkeley and Los Angeles: University of California Press, 1995.

PBS/WGBH. "The Murder of Emmett Till." *American Experience.* www.pbs.org/wgbh/amex/till/filmmore/index.html.

Pease, Ted, and Guido H. Stempel. "Striving to the Top: Views of Minority Newspaper Executives." *Newspaper Research Journal* 11 (1990): 64–79.

Peeples, Melanie. "The Legacy of Medgar Evers." *All Things Considered.* National Public Radio, June 10, 2003. www.npr.org/display_pages/features/feature_1294360.html.

Perkins Margo V. *Autobiography as Activism: Three Black Women of the Sixties.* Jackson: University Press of Mississippi, 2000.

Peterson, V. R. "Jake Lamar: Standing Up to His Demons and Singing the 'Bourgeois Blues.'" Book review. *Essence*, April 1992, 54.

Polishuk, Sandy. "Secrets, Lies, and Misremembering: The Perils of Oral History Interviewing." *Frontiers—A Journal of Women's Studies* 19, no. 3 (1998): 14–23.

Polkinghorne, Donald. *Narrative Knowing and the Human Sciences.* SUNY Series in Philosophy of the Social Sciences. Albany: State University of New York Press, 1988.

Pratt, Mary Louise. "Arts of the Contact Zone." *Profession* 91 (1990): 33–40.

Raybon, Patricia. *My First White Friend: Confessions on Race, Love, and Forgiveness.* New York: Viking, 1996.

Report of the National Advisory Commission on Civil Disorders. New York: Bantam, 1968.

Rivers, Caryl. *Slick Spins and Fractured Facts: How Cultural Myths Distort the News.* New York: Columbia University Press, 1996.

Robert C. Maynard Institute for Journalism Education. "Fault Lines." www.mije.org/faultlines.

Rosenberg, Jonathan, and Zachary Karabell. *Kennedy, Johnson, and the Quest for Justice: The Civil Rights Tapes.* New York: Norton, 2003.

Sayre, Robert F. *American Lives: An Anthology of Autobiographical Writing.* Wisconsin Studies in American Autobiography. Madison: University of Wisconsin Press, 1994.

Schein, Edgar H. *Organizational Culture and Leadership.* 2nd ed. San Francisco: Jossey-Bass, 1992.

Schudson, Michael. *Discovering the News.* New York: BasicBooks, 1978.

Scott, Joan. "Experience." In *Feminists Theorize the Political,* edited by Judith Butler and Joan Scott, 22–40. New York: Routledge, 1992.

Shapiro, Harry. *Eric Clapton: Lost in the Blues.* New York: Da Capo Press, 1992.

Smith, Sidonie. "Autobiographical Manifestos." In *Women, Autobiography, Theory: A Reader,* edited by Sidonie Smith and Julia Watson, 433–40. Wisconsin Studies in American Autobiography. Madison: University of Wisconsin Press, 1998.

Squires, C. R. "Rethinking the Black Public Sphere: An Alternative Vocabulary for Multiple Public Spheres." *Communication Theory* 12, no. 4 (2002): 446–68.

Streitmatter, Rodger. *Raising Her Voice: African-American Women Journalists Who Changed History.* Lexington: University Press of Kentucky, 1994.

Sturrock, John. *The Language of Autobiography: Studies in the First Person Singular.* New York: Cambridge University Press, 1993.

Sylvie, George, and Patricia Dennis Witherspoon. *Time, Change and the American Newspaper.* Lea's Communication Series. Mahwah, NJ: Lawrence Erlbaum Associates, 2002.

Tyson, Timothy B. *Radio Free Dixie: Robert F. Williams & the Roots of Black Power.* Chapel Hill: University of North Carolina Press, 1999.

U.S. Census Bureau. "An Older and More Diverse Nation by Midcentury." Press release, August 14, 2008.

Wallace, Maurice O. *Constructing the Black Masculine: Identity and Ideality in African American Men's Literature and Culture, 1775–1995.* Durham, NC: Duke University Press, 2002.

Wilson, Clint C., Félix Gutiérrez, and Lena M. Chao. *Racism, Sexism, and the Media: The Rise of Class Communication in Multicultural America.* 3rd ed. Thousand Oaks, Calif.: Sage Publications, 2003.

Index

About the Author

Calvin L. Hall (BA, MA, North Carolina State University; PhD, University of North Carolina–Chapel Hill) is assistant professor and faculty fellow in the Department of Communication at Appalachian State University.

A native of Asheville, North Carolina, Hall taught high school English and journalism and served as college media adviser at St. Augustine's College in Raleigh, North Carolina, and also serves as an instructor for the Summer Scholastic Journalism Institute of the North Carolina Scholastic Media Association (NCSMA), headquartered at UNC–Chapel Hill.

He has had work published in the *Journal of Communication Studies*, *Encyclopedia of American Journalism*, and J-Ideas.org, and has reviewed books for *Journalism & Mass Communication Quarterly* and H-Net.org.

Hall is a 2005 Fellow of the Institute for Journalism Excellence, sponsored by the American Society of Newspaper Editors and the John S. and James L. Knight Foundation, and he is a member of the North Carolina Humanities Council.